Atlanta's Oakland Cemetery

Atlanta's
Oakland Cemetery

An Illustrated History and Guide

Ren and Helen Davis

WITH AN INTRODUCTION BY TIMOTHY J. CRIMMINS

PUBLISHED IN ASSOCIATION WITH THE HISTORIC OAKLAND FOUNDATION

THE UNIVERSITY OF GEORGIA PRESS   ATHENS AND LONDON

a Friends Fund publication

*Publication of this work was made possible, in part, by a generous gift
from the University of Georgia Press Friends Fund.*

Designed by Erin Kirk New

Set in Caslon and Whitney

The paper in this book meets the guidelines for permanence and
durability of the Committee on Production Guidelines for Book Longevity
of the Council on Library Resources.

Printed in China

16   15   14   13   12   P   5   4   3   2   1

Library of Congress Cataloging-in-Publication Data

Davis, Ren, 1951–

Atlanta's Oakland Cemetery : an illustrated history and guide /
    by Ren and Helen Davis ; with an introduction by Timothy J. Crimmins.
      p. cm.

Includes bibliographical references and index.

ISBN 978-0-8203-4313-6 (pbk. : alk. paper) —ISBN 0-8203-4313-7 (pbk. : alk. paper)

1. Oakland Cemetery (Atlanta, Ga.) 2. Atlanta (Ga.)—Biography.

3. Atlanta (Ga.)—History—Anecdotes. I. Davis, Helen, 1951– II. Title.

F294.A862O24   2012

363.7′50975823I—dc23   2011044418

British Library Cataloging-in-Publication Data available

AM LAWSON PEEL, JR.
SON OF W.L. AND L.C. PEEL
SEPTEMBER 2, 1882
AUGUST 23, 1895
WE SHALL MEET AGAIN.

UCY MARION COOK
OF WILLIAM LAWSON PEEL
VEMBER 13, 1849
RY 16, 1923

Contents

Preface

WITHIN OAKLAND CEMETERY'S compact forty-eight acres are nearly seventy thousand stories from Atlanta's earliest days as a rowdy railroad camp called Terminus to the international city that now towers above its pastoral grounds. Some of the notable people interred here were civic or business leaders, while others are endeared to our memory for their accomplishments in the arts or athletics. Each, from the humblest former slave or laborer to former mayors, governors, or generals, contributed a thread to the fabric of the great city Atlanta has become.

The historian Franklin Garrett wrote that "old Oakland is Atlanta's most tangible link between the past and present." For anyone seeking to comprehend the city's rich, colorful, and, at times, troubling history, Oakland is a required destination. Beyond local history, the cemetery is a place for quiet reflection, for meandering, and for simply marveling a an unsurpassed collection of funerary art and architecture that reflect both the finest elements of the nineteenth-century rural garden cemetery movement and the evolution of the commemoration and meaning of death in our society.

Whatever your reason for visiting Oakland, we believe the Cemetery's acres will draw you back again and again.

Scope and Limitations

Our purpose in writing and photographing this book was threefold. First was to provide the reader with the story behind the stories, from Oakland's founding in 1850 to the present day. We sought to accomplish this through a short history of the cemetery; an examination of Oakland's role in the rural garden cemetery movement; and an introduction to funerary art, architecture, and symbolism. These elements come together in the walking tours of the cemetery's nine distinctive sections, from the Original Six Acres to Potters' Field.

Second was our effort to capture images of the many facets of Oakland: simple grave markers in the African American Grounds; precisely aligned rows of soldiers' graves in the Confederate Memorial Grounds; closely spaced markers with symbolic details in the Jewish section; and the ornate and elegant mausoleums and monuments that are found throughout the cemetery.

Third was to share the story of the volunteer-driven Historic Oakland Foundation, which works closely with both the City of Atlanta and the local community to preserve and restore these hallowed grounds. This story is told in the section titled "A Gathering Place," where, through many foundation-sponsored events, Oakland's story is shared with the wider world.

While you will find profiles within these pages of several hundred of those who rest at Oakland, this book is not intended to be a comprehensive history of the cemetery. Rather, it is designed to be both an armchair reference as well as an invitation to explore these hallowed grounds and find your own stories within its walls.

Acknowledgments

THIS BOOK would not have been possible without the devoted efforts of many people. Those whose contributions and expertise were most invaluable were David Moore, executive director of the Historic Oakland Foundation; Mary Woodlan, director of volunteers and special events; Libba Grace, the foundation's board chair; Kevin Kuharic, the former director of restoration and landscapes at Oakland and now executive director of the Hotel de Paris Museum in Georgetown, Colorado; and Richard Waterhouse, a funerary-symbolism expert and former volunteer with the foundation who is currently director of the Cahoon Museum of American Art in Cotuit, Massachusetts. We are also grateful to Dustin Hornsby, Oakland's restoration manager and chief technician, who provided access to areas of the cemetery not often open to the public. We wish to recognize other volunteers, including Erin Parr, Cathy Vogel, DL Henderson, and Larry Upthegrove, each of whom generously shared with us his or her knowledge of Oakland and local history; our thanks go also to Oakland Cemetery's sexton, Sam Reed, who provided access to his collection of archival photographs and other materials.

We are also appreciative of those who provided access to archival documents and images. These include the staff of the Kenan Research Center at the Atlanta History Center, especially Sue Verhoef and the late Betsy Rix, who aided us in locating documents and images from the center's collections. Steve Engerrand and Gail DeLoach with the Georgia State Archives provided access to the state's collection of archival images; and Sharon Steele-Smith of the Alfred H. Colquitt Chapter of the United Daughters of the Confederacy shared historical images from the group's archives.

We also wish to express our appreciation to Jamil Zainaldin, the executive director of the Georgia Humanities Council, for his unwavering support for this project from the outset; to Michael Rose of the Atlanta History Center for his thoughtful critique of the manuscript; and to Timothy Crimmins, a professor of heritage preservation at Georgia State University, who reviewed the manuscript, offered valuable insights and recommendations for its improvement, and generously took time to pen the book's introduction.

Finally, a special thank you to everyone at the University of Georgia Press: Nicole Mitchell, director; Laura Sutton, senior acquisitions editor; Jon Davies, managing editor; Sydney DuPre, assistant to the director and development coordinator; Melissa Buchanan, project editor; John McLeod, sales and marketing director; and the immensely talented team of cartographers and layout designers led by Walton Harris and Erin New; thanks also to Kip Keller, freelance copyeditor.

Each person listed above was committed to producing a book that would do justice to historic Oakland Cemetery and those who rest within its walls, as well as to those who are tirelessly dedicated to its preservation for the future. We are indebted to all of them for their able assistance and guidance.

Introduction   TIMOTHY J. CRIMMINS

IN THIS GUIDE to Oakland Cemetery, Ren and Helen Davis bring to life Atlanta's first landscape of remembrance, pointing out that Oakland Cemetery is a miniature version of the city of which it is a part. The novelist William Kennedy captured the relationship between the city of the living and the city of the dead in his 1983 novel *Ironweed* with his keen observation that "the dead, even more than the living, settled down in neighborhoods." As Kennedy's protagonist in the novel, Francis Phelan, travels through a cemetery, he observes its sprawling middle-class neighborhoods, where there were "fields of monuments and cenotaphs of kindred design and striking size, all guarding the privileged dead." As he moves farther on, there appear "acres of truly prestigious death: illustrious men and women, captains of life without their diamonds, furs, carriages, and limousines, but buried in pomp and glory, vaulted in great tombs built like heavenly safe deposit boxes, or parts of the Acropolis." Last came the working classes—"the flowing masses, row upon row of them under simple headstones and simpler crosses."[1]

Oakland Cemetery likewise has its neighborhoods that visibly differentiate prosperity in death as in life, with its "fields of monuments," "great tombs," and "row upon row of simple headstones." By the 1880s, visitors could come to Oakland to see Atlanta in miniature. Those buried there came from the great mansions along Peachtree Street and Capitol Avenue, the cottages along Collins Street, and the shotgun houses in Mechanicsville. There is also the great grassy expanse of Potters' Field, where transients, those without means who lived in boardinghouses and shacks, are buried head by foot under a lawn of grass without commemorative markings. They are as invisible in death as in life. But Oakland Cemetery has significant differences from St. Agnes Cemetery, the real-life location in the Kennedy novel, just as the latter's city, Albany, New York, differs from Atlanta, Georgia. Atlanta's Oakland Cemetery began separating slave from free in the 1850s and continued segregating black from white after the Civil War. St. Agnes was an exclusively Catholic cemetery in a city with a large Catholic population whose working-class and, later, lace-curtain neighborhoods were built by waves of Irish, Italian, and Polish immigrants. Oakland's Catholics are dispersed among their Protestant neighbors. Religious separation in Oakland occurs with the designated Jewish burial area, established when Hebrew congregations purchased areas of the cemetery where they could bury their dead contiguously, according to their laws and customs.

St. Agnes Cemetery describes itself as "consecrated in 1867 in the fashion of a rural cemetery."[2] Oakland Cemetery was established seventeen years earlier, but not in the fashion of a rural cemetery. Even though trendsetting cities like Boston, New York, and Philadelphia had created what came to be known as "rural cemeteries" as early as 1831, the Atlanta City Council, in establishing what came to be known as Oakland Cemetery, just created a municipal burying ground, on land situated to the east of the town's center and beyond its built-up areas. In nineteenth-century New York, Boston, and Atlanta, the provision of burial places was another new municipal service that local governments were forced to provide as a result of their burgeoning populations. The dead became too numerous to be buried in the churchyards that had served colonial-era towns.

Boston, whose population topped seventy thousand in 1830, created a model for addressing the burial needs of its citizens. The city government did not establish a city cemetery; rather, it delegated the task to the not-for-profit sector. Like most large urban centers, Boston had its share of voluntary associations dedicated to promoting the common good, one of which was the Massachusetts Horticultural Society. The society decided to combine its interest in flora with the city's need to bury the dead, so it created a "garden cemetery," a place where the dead would be surrounded with trees, shrubs, and flowers. The place envisioned by society members was to be not just a burial ground visited by the families of the dead, but also a destination for the living of Boston, a place where its residents could come to see a landscaped garden. In 1831, the society purchased seventy-two acres of land across the Charles River four miles west of Boston Common. The key financial question facing the society was how to cover its initial expense of $6,000 and the additional expenses of landscaping the grounds, fencing the property, and constructing an entrance gate and administrative building. The acquisition cost was quickly recouped by the sale of the first hundred lots at $60 each, while additional sales supported land development costs and land purchases that expanded the cemetery to 112 acres by 1850.[3]

In his 1831 address at the dedication of the cemetery, named Mount Auburn, Joseph Story explained that the crowded conditions in Boston, which is surrounded by a harbor and tidal waters, necessitated the location of the cemetery in the countryside, well beyond the city limits. Because of this, he called Mount Auburn a "rural" cemetery, a descriptive that was applied to garden cemeteries in other cities. The Massachusetts Horticultural Society hired Alexander

The map of Mount Auburn Cemetery shows the contours of its carriageways and lanes. Its layout was the model for urban parks and early suburbs in the expanding cities of nineteenth-century America. From James Smillie, *Mount Auburn Illustrated* (New York: R. Martin, 1847).

Wadworth, a civil engineer, to lay out the grounds. Wadworth did this with intersecting, curved, and winding avenues that used the land economically and also produced "the picturesque effect of landscape gardening." Roads made twenty-feet wide for carriages and six-feet wide for foot traffic were lined with ornamental shrubs and flowers. Family lots of three hundred square feet that were sold to the initial purchasers were not expected to lie fallow for long, as Story noted: "It is confidently expected that many of the proprietors will, without delay, proceed to erect upon their lots such monuments and appropriate structures, as will give to the place a part of the solemnity and beauty, which it is destined ultimately to acquire."[4]

Story went on to detail the advantages of such a location:

There are around us all the varied features of her beauty and grandeur—the forest-crowned height; the abrupt acclivity; the sheltered valley; the deep glen; the grassy glade; and the silent grove. Here are the lofty oak, the beech, that "wreathes its old fantastic roots so high," the rustling pine, and the drooping willow. . . . Here is the thick shrubbery to protect and conceal the new-made grave; and there is the wild-flower creeping along the narrow path, and planting its seeds in the upturned earth.[5]

The forested hills overlooking the Charles River served as resting places for deceased Bostonians and as a rural refuge for the living. From James Smillie, *Mount Auburn Illustrated* (New York: R. Martin, 1847).

Story also noted the connection between the cemetery and the city: from the heights of Mount Auburn, visitors could see below them

> the winding Charles with its rippling current. . . . In the distance, the City,—at once the object of our admiration and our love,—rears its proud eminences, its glittering spires, its lofty towers, its graceful mansions, its curling smoke, its crowded haunts of business and pleasure, which speak to the eye, and yet leave a noiseless loneliness on the ear.[6]

By 1840, Mount Auburn had developed a parklike setting, with its specimen trees and shrubs labeled with their Latin names, allowing it to function as the horticultural society's arboretum as well as a cemetery. But it was also a place of art because of the memorials that had been commissioned by the first families of Boston. Three years after the Boston merchant and scientist Amos Binney died in 1847, the *New York Daily Tribune* reported:

> A fine piece of monumental sculpture . . . has just arrived. It was executed in Rome, for the tomb of Dr. Amos Binney of Boston, and will be placed in Mount Auburn Cemetery. Those who have seen the monument in Italy speak in very high terms of its merit as a work of art.[7]

Mount Auburn began as a marriage between the need for burial places beyond the city limits and the desire for a horticultural garden. Its curvilinear streets with wide carriageways attracted the city's increasing numbers of middle and upper classes, who journeyed there for pleasure rides and to show it off to their visitors. They also came to see the works of art in the sculptures and mausoleums erected as memorials to the city's wealthy elite, as well as the more modest statues and tombstones "guarding the privileged dead." Looking back two decades after the establishment of Mount Auburn, the architect and planner Andrew Jackson Downing noted that the first American cemetery was an "idea that took the public mind by storm": "Travelers made pilgrimages to the Athens of New England, solely to see the realization of a resting-place for the dead, at once sacred from profanation, dear to the memory, and captivating to the imagination."[8] As Boston's population expanded across the Charles River toward Cambridge, horse-drawn trolley lines were established to connect Harvard Square with Mount Auburn and the elite suburban neighborhoods that were developing along the route.

Other cities quickly adopted the Mount Auburn model, establishing private societies that purchased rural land, landscaped it, and sold the first lots to a wealthy elite. Philadelphia established Laurel Hill in 1836; Baltimore, Green Mount in 1838; and New York City, Greenwood in 1839.[9] The multiple functions of the rural cemetery fit into an emerging consensus among progressive thinkers about the need for civic improvements in American cities. In his *Rural Essays*, published in 1853, Andrew Jackson Downing argued that the way

The Binney Memorial exemplifies the sculptural works that made Mount Auburn Cemetery a place where visitors could contemplate art as well as nature. From James Smillie, *Mount Auburn Illustrated* (New York: R. Martin, 1847).

to create "a larger and more fraternal spirit in our social life" was to establish "refined places of resort, parks and gardens, galleries, libraries, museums, &c."; such amenities "would soften and humanize the rude, educate and enlighten the ignorant, and give continual enjoyment to the educated."[10] Downing and other urban visionaries viewed garden cemeteries, landscaped parks, libraries, and museums as cultural institutions that would bring order to the rapidly expanding cities of nineteenth-century America.[11]

Downing wrote his *Rural Essays* to promote architecture and public gardens. He recognized how the rural cemetery was a place of contemplation of both nature and art and how its form, without the graves, could be introduced into cities simply as a public park. To do this, Downing encouraged cities to adopt the business model of the rural cemetery for their public gardens, suggesting that "a joint-stock company [be] formed in . . . our cities, for the purpose of providing its inhabitants with the luxury of a public garden," and that its location "be selected with the same judgment which has already been shown by the cemetery companies."[12] The shareholders would have free access to the carriage roads, while other citizens would be admitted by paying a small fee. Downing argued that if thousands would pay to visit P. T. Barnum's American Museum in New York City to see curiosities like stuffed boa constrictors, many more thousands would pay to visit public gardens. Downing's vision of the city linked the cultural values of the rural cemetery with the benefits of other emerging cultural institutions: "The true policy of republics, is to foster the taste for great public libraries, sculpture and picture galleries, parks, and gardens, which all may enjoy, since our institutions wisely forbid the growth of private fortunes sufficient to achieve these desirable results in any other way."[13]

In 1850, when the Atlanta City Council established a municipal cemetery, the city had been incorporated for only four years and had just surpassed the urban population threshold of 2,500 by 75. Its public park was the square in front of the railroad passenger station, and the bulk of the town's developed area lay within three-quarters of a mile of the central square. Mayor Willis Buell and city council members were not interested in paying for a cemetery that would also function as a park; it was to be a burial ground plain and simple. The business model adopted by the city for its new endeavor was the same as that of private cemeteries, with one exception. The city bought land on the east side of the city cheaply and sold it in much smaller cemetery plots at higher prices. The income from the sale of plots not only repaid the price of the land purchase but also enabled the city to appoint a sexton as administrator, acquire additional land for expansion, and construct necessary buildings and a perimeter fence and gateway entrance. The difference between privately operated and municipally run cemeteries was that in the latter, income from land sales went into the city treasury rather than into a fund earmarked for the cemetery. The operational costs of the Atlanta City Cemetery were made a part of the expanding municipal services that Atlanta offered as it grew from a small town of 2,575 in 1850 to a medium-sized city of almost 90,000 in 1900. This guide details the challenges faced by those operating Oakland Cemetery once the flow of cash from the sale of cemetery lots had decreased to a trickle by the 1890s.

Established as a burial ground, the Atlanta City Cemetery acquired greater cultural and material significance because of its hilly location and the course of its development. Twenty-two years after its establishment, with expansions, the erection of monuments, and the growth of a cover of oak trees, the cemetery was renamed Oakland. It had become a garden cemetery with artistic monuments. In May 1871, the *Atlanta Constitution* reported on the raising of "one of the finest monuments in the South" on the Cone plot, where family members had been buried in 1851, 1863, and 1872. It is "fourteen feet high of pure Italian marble, from Carrara, in Italy," and "the base, of Stone Mountain granite, weighs three tons." Capping the monument is a four-and-a-half-foot-tall "life-size figure of Hope with her right hand resting on an anchor, and the left hand placed on her breast"; her clothing drapes from her body "with fine

The addition of the Cone family statue in 1871 along with the maturing oak trees and other flora helped to transform the Atlanta City Cemetery from a simple burial ground into a garden of art and nature.

effect."[14] Even more striking was the Austell mausoleum, which was completed in 1883 and located "near the center of the cemetery, on one of its highest knolls, commanding a fine view of the entire grounds and of the city." The monument was designed to impress: "Its appearance is solemnly imposing and attracts the eye as soon as one enters the gates." The forty-foot-high edifice has a granite exterior, an interior lined with Italian marble, and room for twenty-eight bodies, three of which are sized for children.[15]

Atlantans were aware of what a rural cemetery looked like. An 1869 correspondent from Atlanta reported in the *Atlanta Constitution* of a visit to "that earthly paradise Mount Auburn Cemetery." Visitors could travel there by horse-drawn trolleys, described by the correspondent as "those Northern luxuries," that left Harvard square every fifteen minutes.[16] When the Atlanta developers Richard Peters and George Washington Adair established the city's first mule-drawn trolley lines four years later, the line to the east along Decatur Street ended at Oakland Cemetery, making it a destination for those who wished to view the art and architecture being erected there. But in the decade following the Civil War, visits to Oakland Cemetery were less likely to be for its parklike setting than for its function as a site of remembrance.

As this guide demonstrates, after the Civil War, in contrast to rural cemeteries in the North, Oakland Cemetery became the principal place in Atlanta of mourning and memorialization of those who had died defending the Confederacy. No sooner had Atlanta begun to rebuild itself in the aftermath of its destruction in 1864 than women began to repair the damage to the graves of those buried there during the Atlanta Campaign. In addition, they gathered the remains of soldiers who had been buried in shallow graves on the battlefields of Peachtree Creek, East Atlanta, and Ezra Church and reinterred them in Oakland. Once the Atlanta Ladies Memorial Association (ALMA), the organization of women who spearheaded the refurbishment and expansion of the section of the cemetery dedicated to the Confederate dead, had begun its initial effort, it instituted what became an annual memorial event to honor what were called the fallen heroes.

It was particularly galling to these women that the federal government paid for the costs of interring and memorializing the Union dead, while the Confederate fallen were left untended on the battlefields where they had died. For them, the tombstones that they placed over the Confederate graves in Oakland had special meaning. Mrs. George T. Fry, the secretary of ALMA, put this succinctly in an 1890 Confederate Memorial Day address in which she had a group of children ask the question: "'What mean these [Confederate head] stones?'" Her answer was:

Newspaper articles kept nineteenth-century Atlantans up to date on the amenities of cities like Boston, where a visitor to the famous Mount Auburn Cemetery detailed the picturesque scenery and the trolley cars that made it easily accessible to urbanites. From James Smillie, *Mount Auburn Illustrated* (New York: R. Martin, 1847).

Tell them that these are the graves of patriot heroes, who in the defense of southern rights, honor, constitutional government and liberty, fell defeated. . . . That the bodies of the victorious slain were honorably entombed by the government, that two such national cemeteries are located in Georgia. While the bodies of these patriot martyrs were left to lie in the trenches around this city, until the noble impoverished women worked for and begged the money to pay the cost of removing them, stood by the trenches while they were being disinterred, and with loving hands, gave them a Christian Burial. Although it took them a quarter of a century to overcome these obstacles, they worked with untiring energy, until they had built a monument of Georgia's own granite, and paid for the stones that marked their soldiers' graves.[17]

In 1870, when the women of ALMA began raising funds to erect a great "monument of Georgia's own granite" as a memorial to the Confederate dead in Atlanta, there was a disagreement about whether it should be placed in Oakland Cemetery, where the dead were interred, or in the heart of Atlanta. The *Atlanta Constitution* editorialized that the cemetery location "in the midst of the graves of the dead will perpetuate the sanctity of their resting-place; preserve it from desecration, and seal their title to undisturbed possession of the sacred spot in all time to come." It would have the added benefit of attracting visitors to the cemetery, encouraging "the proper preservation and ornamentation of the graves and grounds." On the other hand, the editor went on, if "the monument is designed chiefly to gratify the pride of the living and as an ornament to our town," then it should be placed at the center of the city, where it would honor all the dead of Georgia, not just those buried in Oakland. After much debate, Oakland and the Atlanta-area fallen won out.[18] In October 1870, the cornerstone of the monument was laid by ALMA, making Oakland Cemetery *the* site in Atlanta of Confederate memorialization for more than a century.

Dedicated in 1874, the Confederate Obelisk in Oakland Cemetery became the backdrop of the annual Confederate Memorial Day celebrations for Atlanta, which grew into major political and cultural events. Twenty-two years later, nearly ten thousand people gathered in the cemetery, five thousand of whom crowded around the monument after a parade from Peachtree Street witnessed by thousands more. The parade included mounted police, the Governor's Horse Guards, the United States Army Fifth Regiment infantry band and Gatling gun platoon, the Lyceum band, a police battalion, the Gate City Guard escorting Confederate veterans, the Hibernian association, the Sons of Confederate Veterans mounted on horses, carriages carrying members of ALMA, and carriages containing the orator, public officials, and leading citizens.[19]

Speeches given by prominent Georgians at the Confederate Memorial Day celebrations preached the Lost Cause ideology that idealized the Confederacy and the Old South.[20] In his 1896 oration, U.S. Attorney Dupont Guerry, a

The Confederate Obelisk was dedicated in 1874 in the heart of the section of the Confederate dead, where it served as a destination for Atlanta's annual Confederate Memorial Day parades into the 1950s.

former state senator who would run unsuccessfully for governor in 1902 and serve as president of Wesleyan Female College in Macon from 1903 to 1909, began by saying that his purpose was to

> publicly declare to mankind and to God our steadfast devotion and undying gratitude to the brave men who fought and died for us; commemorate in praise and song, in prayers and tears their heroic deeds and sufferings and testify anew to our faith in the purity, patriotism and philanthropy of their motives and purposes.

Guerry continued with an account of the "superior wisdom of our confederate ancestors" by listing a number of articles in the Confederate constitution that were being considered by the United States Congress, including civil service reform and the executive power of a line-item veto. He also addressed the iconography of national remembrance:

> We join them [Northerners] in their reverence for Abraham Lincoln as the exponent of their triumphal statesmanship, and in their admiration for Grant as the leader of their victorious Army of the Potomac. But if they cannot join us in our reverence for Jefferson Davis as the chieftain of our lost confederacy, and in our admiration for Robert Edward Lee as the captain of our army of northern Virginia, we must enjoy these privileges without them. Our children and our children's children will continue to do so down the ages.[21]

In the course of the twentieth century, the horse-drawn carriages of the Confederate Memorial Day parade to Oakland were replaced by automobiles and the Lost Cause ideology hardened into dogma. The overwhelming sense of loss that had motivated ALMA to make Oakland Cemetery a site for memory and bereavement faded away as the annual Confederate Memorial Day event became an occasion for defending the white southern way of life. Eugene Talmadge, a former governor, found this out the hard way. As a Georgia politician, he used the Lost Cause ideology to justify his advocacy of segregation, but in 1936 in a speech at Lincoln's tomb in Illinois, he tried to enlist the Republican Lincoln in support of his criticism of the Democrat Franklin Roosevelt: "Would that we had a man like Abraham Lincoln in the White House today. If we did, he would never allow a brain truster's creed to teach the doctrine that you can boon-doggle yourself back to prosperity." Talmadge hoped his speech would help him win the Republican nomination for president, but it backfired with his southern base of support. Talmadge returned to Georgia to rally his supporters by speaking even more vociferously for white supremacy.[22]

Two years later, when Talmadge was invited to deliver the keynote address at the Confederate Memorial Day celebration in Oakland Cemetery, his comment about Lincoln came back to haunt him. The United Confederate Veterans protested his selection as speaker, saying that because of his speech advocating a new Lincoln in the White House, "he is not the proper person to speak over their dead comrades at any time." The United Daughters of the Confederacy organized a boycott of the event. Three chapters refused to participate; two chapters that had cars in the parade instructed their drivers to turn away before entering the cemetery. It was clear that the reconciliatory sentiment of Dupont Guerry's 1896 oration at Oakland—claiming that southerners joined northerners in their reverence for Lincoln—no longer held sway.[23]

In the course of the twentieth century, other memorial sites competed with Oakland to be the location in Atlanta where the Lost Cause of the Confederacy would be most honored. After the death of the former Confederate general and Georgia governor John Brown Gordon in January 1904, Atlanta's civic leaders raised funds to build a memorial in his honor. The statue that was commissioned and erected on the grounds of the Georgia Capitol depicted Gordon's face as it was when he was an elderly statesman, but his body was clothed in his Confederate uniform and mounted on his favorite horse during the Civil War. At the dedication ceremony in May 1907, Governor Terrell called for the placement of a second statue, honoring the Georgia Confederate general James Longstreet, and a third, honoring the common soldier. The following speaker, Joe Hall from Macon, proposed a fourth statue, one of General Robert E. Lee. A Southern Monuments Commission was established to advance the plan to surround the Georgia Capitol with Confederate memorial statues, but the high cost of the project doomed it to failure.[24]

In the early decades of the twentieth century, Oakland remained the site of Confederate memorialization. ALMA attracted large crowds for its annual parade down Peachtree Street to Whitehall Street to Hunter Street to Oakland for Confederate Memorial Day speeches. The *Atlanta Constitution* reported in 1938 that notwithstanding the boycott called because Eugene Talmadge was speaking, there was a large and lively parade: "Beneath the blue canopy of southern skies more than 100 patriotic and civic organizations did join in honoring the Confederate soldiers—both living and dead. Marching to the stirring strains of 'Dixie,' the line of marchers paraded through downtown Atlanta and then proceeded to the Oakland cemetery."[25]

The annual parade to Oakland Cemetery to celebrate Confederate Memorial Day continued into the 1950s. As metropolitan Atlanta began its rapid expansion in the post–World War II period, the push to complete the Stone Mountain memorial carving, which had been promoted by the United Daughters of the

Confederacy since 1915, began to build momentum. In the 1910s and 1920s, the City of Atlanta had supported two efforts to carve the face of the mountain, and in the 1930s had pushed for the construction of [Confederate] Memorial Drive, which ran from the Capitol, past Oakland Cemetery, and on to Stone Mountain. After the completion in 1971 of the Stone Mountain carving, which depicts the Lost Cause icons Robert E. Lee, Jefferson Davis, and Stonewall Jackson, and with the strengthening of the civil rights movement in the city in the 1960s, the annual Confederate Memorial Day parade to Oakland Cemetery was discontinued. Politicians no longer vied to speak at ceremonies memorializing the Lost Cause, and the annual Confederate Memorial Day event at Oakland Cemetery diminished in size. A new memorialization of the civil rights movement began to take precedence. After the death of Martin Luther King Jr., King's birthday became, for late twentieth- and early twenty-first-century Atlanta, what Confederate Memorial Day had been in the hundred years after the Civil War. King Day celebrations at Ebenezer Baptist Church attract nationally prominent speakers who are as willing to be associated with the successful civil rights movement as were Georgia and southern political leaders who had come to Oakland Cemetery for Confederate Memorial Day celebrations.

The Confederate Memorial Day ceremonies were not the only events that attracted large crowds to Oakland cemetery in the late nineteenth century. When Georgia governor Alexander Stephens, a former vice president of the Confederacy, died in office in March 1883, his remains were carried to Oakland Cemetery in what the newspaper described as "the grandest funeral march ever seen in Georgia." In the parade of carriages, military bands played the "Death March" as the procession, which stretched from the Capitol to the cemetery, moved through vast crowds along the route. Stephens's remains were placed in the Cotting family vault. According to the newspaper: "The hearse carrying the body stopped at the back of the vault and pall bearers came forward to bear the remains . . . to their final resting place." John W. Beckwith, the Episcopal bishop of Georgia, then conducted a short ceremony as the hushed crowd stood hatless. Then the cemetery sexton closed the door of the vault, and the military bands began their departure, again playing the "Death March."[26] But Stephens's final resting place was not to be Oakland Cemetery. Two years later, his casket was relocated to Crawfordville to be placed beneath a memorial statue at his home, Liberty Hall (now Alexander Stephens State Park).[27]

In December 1889, after the sudden death of *Atlanta Constitution* editor Henry Grady, Oakland Cemetery was again the site of a great public burial service. A long procession of twenty-four carriages formed on Peachtree Street to accompany Grady's remains to Oakland. At the head was a carriage carrying Governor John Gordon, Chief Justice Logan E. Bleckley of the Georgia

Supreme Court, Mayor J. T. Glenn of Atlanta, and former governor Henry McDaniel. Throngs of people four to five deep watched the procession from the sidewalk. The carriages filled the roads in the cemetery, and the crowds spilled over the grounds at the base of the hill where Grady was to be interred. The family of John T. Grant offered their mausoleum as a temporary resting place until a permanent burial site could be prepared. There was but a very short ceremony when Grady's remains were carried by pallbearers into the vault as thousands looked on in hushed silence. At the conclusion of the interment, the reporter describing the event waxed poetic in depicting the moment: "The great master of the day sank down in the west in a golden glory just as this great master of men was laid to sleep in his golden prime, and the stars came out one by one in the heavens, as the souls who loved him left him to God."[28] Grady's remains were relocated without fanfare two years later to the newly erected Grady family vault in Westview Cemetery.[29]

Grady's reinterment in Westview Cemetery signaled a profound change for Oakland Cemetery. Forty years after it was established, the cemetery was running out of plots to sell. Atlanta was outgrowing its first cemetery and had sufficient population to support additional burial grounds. At this point, the city wisely opted not to expand its cemetery operations, leaving the task up to the private sector. In 1884, the city authorized a private corporation to establish a whites-only cemetery on the west side of the city. Two years later, at the behest of black community leaders, the city authorized another corporation to establish South-View for African American burials. The erection of the Grady family vault in the newly established Westview Cemetery meant that the era of mausoleum building in Oakland Cemetery was coming to an end. Oakland would continue to be a place of interment and monument building for families who owned lots and vaults, but from the mid-1880s, it was to be but one of the growing city's cemeteries.

The great vaults of the Grant, Cotting, and Austell families, along with the Confederate Memorial, created a mini-skyline in Oakland that was masked from afar from the taller cover of oak trees. But by the 1890s, the city of the dead mirrored the city of the living. The original street pattern of the earliest sections of Oakland followed the north-south, east-west grid of Atlanta's streets, and this was continued through expansions all the way to the eastern boundary of the cemetery at Boulevard. But in the northern sections of Oakland, planners introduced curvilinear streets that were similar to the byways of garden cemeteries and also to the avenues in two nearby developments: Grant Park, the city's first landscaped suburban park, and Inman Park, Atlanta's first planned picturesque suburb.

The picturesque garden landscape shared by the cemetery, the public park, and the planned suburb was the product of the expansion of the American city in the nineteenth century. As rural cemeteries became places for exurban recreation, urban visionaries like Andrew Jackson Downing advocated their replication within the limits of expanding cities as landscaped parks for recreation and renewal—and without the burial function. The renowned landscape architect and urban visionary Frederick Law Olmsted put this into practice with his winning design for Central Park in New York City, which was constructed between 1857 and 1870. After his work designing Central Park, Olmsted incorporated the garden qualities seen in both rural cemeteries and public parks into his conception of ideal suburban developments. Olmsted's concept was to nestle homes along curvilinear streets with setbacks that allowed for graceful front lawns, shrubbery, flower beds, and tree-lined streets. The landscape he created gave the well-to-do residents of the planned suburbs the feeling of living in the country, but they also had urban services like water, sewer, gas, and, later, electricity. Olmsted's first suburb was his 1868 plan for the community of Riverside, Illinois, which was located on a commuter railroad line nine miles west of Chicago.

America's larger urban centers incorporated the garden qualities of the cemetery, park, and suburb into their expanding perimeters from the 1830s to the 1870s. It was in the 1880s that Atlanta became large enough to support these developments, and Oakland Cemetery led the way. By the 1880s, it had become more than a place of Civil War memorialization or of occasional grand funerals for important public figures. With its canopy of trees, its variations in topography, its shrubbery and flowers, and the art and architecture of its sculpture and mausoleums, Oakland had become a recreational destination. On a fine spring Sunday in April 1882, the *Atlanta Constitution* reported that there were throngs of people at the three city parks: the small park next to city hall (on the site of what is now the Capitol), Ponce de Leon Springs (a privately operated amusement park on Ponce de Leon Avenue across from the old Sears), and Oakland Cemetery. So great was the demand to get to Oakland that the trolley company put in a double line of streetcars. A reporter noted of the cemetery's landscaping that the "flowers are looking unusually lovely now, while the evergreen hedges are as fresh in their pretty green as imagination can picture."[30] The following April, the newspaper noted that when visitors returning north from winter stays in Florida stopped for a few days in Atlanta, they would spend an hour or two in Oakland amidst its "winding walks, its vine encircled tombs, it creeping myrtle vines, its twining sweet brier, its lovely violets, and its soft music stealing upon the whispering breeze."[31]

In 1882, Oakland Cemetery was the only public place in Atlanta with garden-park landscaping. There were two other suburban destinations for recreation: Ponce de Leon Springs and Oglethorpe Park. Ponce de Leon Springs was more an entertainment venue, with rides, a picnic pavilion, and an artificial lake for swimming. It was located at the end of the mule-drawn trolley line, about two miles northeast of the downtown. Oglethorpe Park was located on the western trolley line that ran along Marietta Street. In 1881, the International Cotton Exposition constructed its major attraction, the Exposition Cotton Mill, in the park. After the fair, the city sold the park to the Cotton Mill owners for $15,000, significantly reducing the city's available parkland. The following year, Lemuel P. Grant, who was building a steam-dummy trolley line to run southeast from downtown to his large landholdings in what is now the Grant Park neighborhood, deeded to the city the land for a landscaped park. Using funds from the sale of Oglethorpe Park, the city paid for roads and walkways through the wooded valleys of this suburban land, creating Atlanta's first garden park. By the fall of 1884, the hundred-acre Grant Park was described as

> well timbered, presenting a beautiful array of oak, hickory, chestnut and pine. The land is undulated gradually rising from the entrance to a fine height and a commanding view of the eastern boundary. The hills, nooks and hollows give a variety which art can make very attractive. . . . The wide avenues have been skillfully laid and afford a drive through every portion of the grounds. . . . There are a half dozen pretty woodland ways.[32]

Grant Park opened in 1883 as Atlanta's first landscaped park where wooded hills and grassy fields with curving roads and pedestrian lanes gave the picturesque appearance of the garden cemetery.

So from the mid-1880s, Atlanta had two garden landscapes to visit: Oakland Cemetery and Grant Park. Both were located to the east of the downtown. They were joined in the late 1880s by the city's first planned garden suburb, Inman Park, which was located a half mile east of the cemetery and north of the Georgia Railroad tracks and DeKalb Avenue. Joel Hurt had his suburban property laid out with curvilinear tree-lined streets, grassy and wooded linear parks, and setbacks for residences so that front and side yards could be landscaped with trees, shrubs, and flowers. Trained as a civil engineer, Hurt laid out the neighborhood in the style developed by Frederick Law Olmsted twenty years earlier. He hired the landscape architect Joseph Forsyth Johnson to direct the landscaping of the parks and streets, an operation that included the planting of more than seven hundred trees. Hurt made this suburban land available for residential development by constructing the city's first electric trolley line, which ran from Five Points along Edgewood Avenue to the suburb. The trolley route made Inman Park a destination point for the families who lived there

The lake and newly planted trees and shrubs of Springvale Park in the heart of Inman Park created a picturesque setting for suburban houses in the 1890s.

and the domestic workers who worked there, and it also made it possible for Atlantans from other parts of the city to journey there to take advantage of its parklike qualities. In 1890, the *Constitution* reported that the "natural beauty of the park has made it quite a popular Sunday resort."[33]

Oakland Cemetery, Inman Park, and Grant Park are part of the historic landscape produced in Atlanta during its nineteenth-century development. All share the picturesque landscaping that nineteenth-century visionaries like Olmsted and Downing thought would ameliorate the crowded conditions created by rapidly growing cities. They thought that these designed spaces would, in Downing's words: "soften and humanize the rude, educate and enlighten the ignorant, and give continual enjoyment to the educated."[34] Yet in the South in general and Atlanta in particular, slavery was replaced by a color line designed to restrict the movements of African Americans and keep them in subservient positions. As a result, poorly educated blacks were restricted from using parks and cemeteries for enlightenment, while those who were educated could not go there for continual enjoyment. And although houses in Inman Park were available only to white purchasers, they contained attic and basement rooms for black domestic workers, who were not among those strolling the sidewalks and parks, unless they were in attendance on the white children of their employers. The same was true of Grant Park, where the official policy was that African Americans were to be admitted only when accompanying the children of white parents.

Although blacks attended the burials of relatives in Oakland and visited their graves in the colored section of the cemetery, they could not stroll its lanes on the weekend or use the comfort stations erected for white visitors. But within the strictures of the color line, African Americans were a presence in Oakland Cemetery. Many prominent families owned burial plots that attracted large crowds when their members passed. In early February 1936, upon the death of Charles A. Faison, who had worked at the Herndon Barber Shop at 66 Peachtree Street for almost a half a century and had been a member of the Masons, John Wesley Dobbs called for an escort of Masons to accompany the body from the church to Oakland for interment. Later that month, the *Atlanta Daily World* published a picture taken in "historic Oakland cemetery" of five bishops from the African Methodist Episcopal church; W. A. Fountain Jr., the president of Morris Brown College; and Henry Howard, the "son of the late David T. Howard, the noted pioneer southern undertaker," all at the burial of Bishop H. Blanton Parks. The paper reported on a number of pilgrimages to Oakland for commemorative ceremonies at the graves of noted African Americans. In June 1934 a motorcade stopped in the cemetery to lay a wreath on the grave of W. H. Butler, who had been grand master of the Prince

Hall Masons of Georgia from 1901 to 1932. In January 1938, black Boy Scouts from the segregated troops of the Atlanta Area Council "made a pilgrimage" to Butler's grave. In June 1940, when the Prince Hall Masons Building was dedicated, the ceremonies included a visit to Oakland to lay a wreath on Butler's grave. The grave of Bishop W. J. Gaines, a founder of Morris Brown College, was also a site of commemoration. In August 1935, a hundred-car motorcade of members of the African Methodist Episcopal Church stopped at his grave for a remembrance ceremony.[35]

This guide details how African American burial places in the cemetery were relocated twice to make room for additional white burials. Blacks were not permitted to purchase plots or be buried anywhere in the cemetery except in the area designated as colored. The guide explains that the two African Americans who are buried in the white section of the cemetery required specific exemptions requested by white families. In each case, those interred were presented as "faithful" servants whom the white families wished to have in nearby attendance in death as they had been in life.

The dissolution of the color line has transformed modern Atlanta. No longer are public parks segregated or houses in historic neighborhoods restricted to white purchasers. The burial patterns in Oakland Cemetery reflect the segregated past of the city, but as the guide points out, former mayor Maynard Jackson changed that in 2003. Jackson, who broke the color line in life when he became Atlanta's first black mayor, broke the color line in death when he became the first African American to be buried in an area for the white dead.

Maynard Jackson broke the color line in life and in death. In 1973 he was the first African American elected as mayor of Atlanta; thirty years later, he was the first black to be buried in a section of the cemetery that had been restricted to whites.

A view of Oakland's highest hill reveals a cemetery skyline of monuments to nineteenth-century city builders against the backdrop of late twentieth-century skyscrapers.

The *Atlanta Constitution* reported that Mayor Shirley Franklin arranged this by offering Jackson's family a city-owned plot. The report goes on to note the interment of Jackson in Oakland was "richly symbolic, if not a bit ironic, considering that the cemetery is closely identified with the Old South." But Maynard Jackson represents the new Atlanta and the twenty-first-century South. He now lies "at the base of a sloping hill near the cemetery's arched brick entranceway . . . resting under a 150-year-old oak" and facing the "downtown skyline filled with Atlanta's signature skyscrapers, many of which were built on his watch."[36]

When visitors today walk the lanes of Oakland, they can enjoy the garden landscape that it shares with Inman Park and Grant Park, listen for the silent echoes of crowds attending the burials of Henry Grady or Alexander Stephens, see the Confederate Obelisk where thousands gathered annually for Confederate Memorial Day speeches advancing the Lost Cause ideology, look down the avenues where motorcades came to honor Masonic Grand Master W. H. Butler and Morris Brown College founder Bishop W. J. Gaines, and view the neighborhoods of rich and poor, black and white, that mirror the divides in nineteenth- and early twentieth-century Atlanta. In this regard the cemetery is a time capsule of the city's past, but not a frozen past. Oakland gives the opportunity for visitors to see the city of today as well. From its hills, visitors can look west and contemplate the downtown skyline, which signals Atlanta's late twentieth-century expansion into a metropolitan region, and look east to the towering industrial buildings of Fulton Bag and Cotton Mills, which have been converted to apartment living, a sign of the ongoing revitalization of the city's in-town neighborhoods.

One

From Atlanta Cemetery to Historic Oakland

A Short History

Within the confines of those brick and stone walls there's hardly a chapter of our city's history that cannot be told.

DONALD R. ROONEY,
Atlanta History Center

TUCKED BENEATH the Atlanta skyline and nearly hidden behind century-old walls are the grounds of historic Oakland Cemetery, the final resting place for nearly seventy thousand people. Like an island in the midst of the bustling city, this tranquil landscape evolved from a utilitarian municipal graveyard to an outstanding example of the rural garden cemeteries that gained popularity during the nineteenth century.

In many ways, the history of Oakland is Atlanta's story in microcosm. From the resting places of the city's pioneer settlers to the soaring Confederate Monument surrounded by soldiers' graves; from the elegant mausoleums and monuments of those who rebuilt the city after the Civil War to the simple stones marking the graves of former slaves, each is a thread woven into the tapestry of Atlanta's rich history.

Establishing the Atlanta City Cemetery

In 1837, a zero milepost was driven into the ground at the planned juncture of the Georgia and Central of Georgia railroads, with the newly chartered Western and Atlantic Railroad being constructed to link the site with Ross's Landing on the Tennessee River (present-day Chattanooga, Tennessee). Within five years, the rowdy construction camp of Terminus would grow into the village of Marthasville, named for Martha Lumpkin, the daughter of Governor Wilson Lumpkin (she is interred in Oakland Cemetery's Original Six Acres). Despite predictions that the railroad hamlet would never amount to more than a way station, settlers continued to arrive, and the burgeoning town adopted the name "Atlanta" in late 1845.

As the hub of an expanding railroad network, Atlanta soon became a regional transportation center, its population exceeding 2,500 in 1849. That year, the city council recognized that the growing city had a problem. Atlanta's only public burial ground, a small lot on Peachtree Road (between present-day Harris and Baker Streets) was already overcrowded and sat in the path of future development. It had to be closed, and the bodies exhumed and relocated. At its October 1849 meeting, the council appointed a committee to "contract for a suitable graveyard for the city."[1]

In June 1850, after reviewing possible sites within the city for several months and finding nothing suitable or affordable, Mayor Willis Buell and the council selected property just east of the town's boundary and south of the Georgia Railroad tracks. The six-acre tract of rolling farmland (lots 19, 20, 21, 22, 28, and 29 of land lot 45 of the fourteenth district of DeKalb County) was purchased from Alfred W. Wooding for seventy-five dollars an acre and chartered as the "Atlanta Cemetery."[2] Wooding's wife, Agnes, who had recently died and was interred in a plot of land sold to the city, became the first inhabitant of the new burial ground.

Grave of Dr. James Nissen, Oakland's first direct interment

The property as first acquired was later described in the minutes of the Atlanta City Council from July 3, 1857: "The unimproved acreage consisted of six city lots with an alley running through and lay just south of the Georgia Railroad. The Decatur Road was just across the tracks and Elmore and Read Streets ran north from the tract to the roadbed. Holcombe Street was the northern boundary of the land which was hilly and offered a vantage of the growing town to the west."[3]

Even before the property was surveyed into burial lots, the first bodies were exhumed from the old Peachtree graveyard and relocated to unmarked sites in the new cemetery. According to local lore, the new cemetery's first direct interment was the body of Dr. James Nissen, a physician who died in the care of pioneer Atlanta doctor, Dr. Noel P. P. D'Alvigny, while visiting Atlanta. It has been recounted that Nissen, fearful of being buried alive (not an uncommon phobia in those days), asked D'Alvigny to sever his jugular vein before the casket was closed. Nissen's fading tombstone (and a modern tablet recounting the story) may be seen near the cemetery's main entrance.

In February 1851, Oliver Hazard Perry Conant was hired as cemetery sexton. A month later, the council contracted for the sale of wood from the cemetery site and commissioned Councilman John T. Humphries to construct a post-and-plank fence around the property and lay out lots. In April, the first twenty lots were sold for ten dollars each.

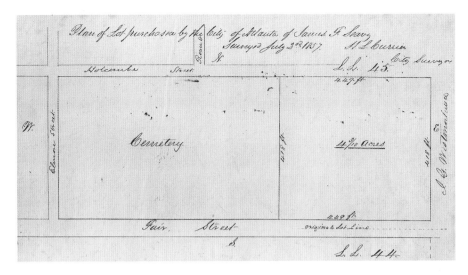

The following year, the city council reported that there remained an urgent need for a thorough survey of the cemetery ground and for the assignment of sections segregated by race. Meeting minutes also noted that more land should be designated for pauper and travelers' interments. When the original six acres of Oakland were laid out in 1850, space was set aside in the northeastern corner, far from the private lots and public grounds, for the segregated interment of slaves and free blacks. The first recorded black burial was the interment of a fourteen-year-old boy on February 10, 1853. During the next dozen years, nearly nine hundred more bodies, many in unmarked graves, were interred in what was commonly called "Slave Square." Records of slave burials are incomplete, often listing the full name of the slave's owner and only a first name of the deceased, with the notation "Negro."

In 1853, Green Pilgrim replaced Conant as sexton, and the number of burials continued to increase as the city grew. By 1857, the availability of lots was dwindling, so four acres of sloping land on the eastern border of the cemetery (the area now called Child Square) were acquired from a local landowner, James Seavy.

Despite these additions, Mayor Luther J. Glenn reported in 1859 that the grounds were in poor condition, vandalism was a growing problem, and immediate improvements were still needed. Within the next year, the remaining bodies from the old Peachtree Road burial ground were finally reinterred in the new cemetery. In December 1860, the city sold six lots to David Mayer, the president of the Hebrew Benevolent Association (predecessor of the Hebrew Benevolent Congregation), for Jewish burials. As

Atlanta's Jewish population grew, additional Jewish burial spaces would be set aside in 1878 and 1892. Many of the gravestones in the Jewish sections are inscribed in Hebrew. Eric Goldstein, a professor of Jewish Studies at Emory University, translated many of the inscriptions into English. These translation documents are housed in the archives of Atlanta's Breman Jewish Heritage and Holocaust Museum.

Given the existence of slavery and rigid ethnic divisions in the early to mid-nineteenth century, the Atlanta City Cemetery's plans to permit black interments and to set aside space for the establishment of a distinct Jewish burial ground were in marked contrast to the prevailing racial, religious, and cultural segregation practiced in municipal graveyards in both the North and the South. In her book *The American Resting Place: Four Hundred Years of History through Our Cemeteries and Burial Grounds*, Marilyn Yalom notes that in many cemeteries of that period, "religious and ethnic prejudice prevailed in underground America, just as it prevailed aboveground."[4]

Old Jewish section at Oakland, established 1860

The Civil War

In November 1860, Abraham Lincoln, a Republican, was elected to the presidency without a single Atlantan's vote. Sectional tensions over states' rights and slavery grew more intense following South Carolina's secession from the Union in December. A month later, on January 19, 1861, Georgia joined the newly formed Confederate States of America. With the outbreak of the Civil War in April of that year, Atlanta became a major industrial and transportation center for the Confederacy, making it a target for Union troops.

In April 1862, Union raiders led by James J. Andrews stole the Western and Atlantic Railroad's engine, "General," at Big Shanty (Kennesaw), with plans to travel north and destroy the vital railroad line to Chattanooga. With the crew of the "General" (the engineer, Jeff Cain; the conductor, William Fuller; and the foreman, Anthony Murphy) in desperate pursuit aboard the "Texas," the raiders were captured near Ringgold, Georgia, and returned to Atlanta. After trial as spies, Andrews and seven raiders were hanged and six others were imprisoned. Andrews was executed near present-day Midtown Atlanta and

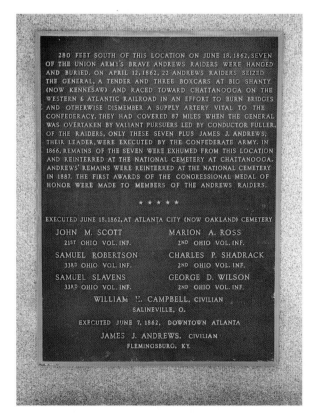

Andrews' Raiders historical tablet at Oakland

buried nearby; the others were put to death in a wooded area south of Decatur Road and buried in the Atlanta Cemetery. Six of the raiders would become the first recipients of the newly created Medal of Honor. After the war, all the bodies of those executed would be relocated to the National Cemetery in Chattanooga, Tennessee, beside a replica of the "General." Later, Fuller, Cain, and Murphy would each be interred in Oakland Cemetery.

Opposite: Captain William Fuller's grave and obelisk

As the war progressed, Atlanta took on a critical role as a major medical center. According to an account in *Barnwell's Atlanta City Directory and Stranger's Guide* (1867),

> Great numbers of sick and wounded soldiers daily arriving at the Passenger Depot, were met by the ladies of the first families, with baskets filled with such delicacies, &c, as were most needed by them. It is estimated that, from time to time, during the war, there were in hospital at this place, not less than 80,000 Confederate soldiers, and that of this number about 5,000 died; 4,600 [the actual number was closer to 3,900] of whom were buried in the City Cemetery. There were probably 2,500 Federals, also in hospital at this place, about 150 of whom were buried in the City Cemetery.[5]

In her book, *This Republic of Suffering: Death and the American Civil War*, the historian Drew Gilpin Faust describes the enormous strains from the mounting casualties as "the capacities of existing cemeteries in towns like Richmond and Atlanta were taxed, then exceeded, as communities struggled to provide graves for the escalating number of the fallen."[6]

Following the fighting at Chickamauga and Chattanooga (September–November 1863), southbound trains brought thousands more wounded and ill soldiers to Atlanta's Gate City Hospital, the Fairground Hospitals across the road from the cemetery, and nearly thirty other makeshift hospitals across the city and surrounding communities. Atlanta's doctors and military physicians labored under extraordinarily difficult conditions, often lacking the supplies and medicines needed to ease their patients' suffering. Sexton Pilgrim recorded the burial of about two hundred soldiers during the third quarter of 1863, with interments increasing to nearly seven hundred following the carnage at Chickamauga, Lookout Mountain, and Missionary Ridge.

Overworked laborers did not discriminate among Confederate or Union dead, interring the bodies in a common area in the cemetery. This prompted an October 24, 1863, letter to Dr. J. P. Logan, the chief surgeon for the Atlanta hospitals, from an angry Confederate colonel, Moses Hannibal Wright. He

Union graves with American flags

wrote, "This is all wrong—unkind and ungenerous—showing a want of that feeling for our Brothers which should be most kind in every living breast—and a disregard for them reflecting only discredit on us all."[7]

Despite such protests, Union casualties continued to be buried alongside Confederate. After the war, most of the Union dead were removed for reinterment in their home states or in the National Cemetery in Chattanooga. However, sixteen Union soldiers who died in Atlanta hospitals in 1862 remain interred in the Confederate Grounds at Oakland, and their distinctive, rounded gravestones may be seen in Section C.

With available burial space rapidly diminishing, the city council asked the Confederate government to purchase adjacent property and deed it to the city, but no action took place. Eventually, the city purchased several acres of rolling, wooded land east of the cemetery from Dr. John G. Westmoreland for $30,000 and requested that the Confederate government reimburse one-sixth of the price. Again, there was no response. Finally, the city reclaimed funds collected from the sale of wood that had been cut from the property by the Confederate government. Interestingly, despite all these efforts, no soldiers would be buried in this expanded section of the cemetery.

Nonetheless, by the spring of 1864, additional burials had nearly filled the additional land, and the city council prepared another petition asking the Confederate government to purchase more land. This time it was not the government that brought negotiations to a halt—it was Major General William Tecumseh Sherman of the United States Army.

In July 1864, as the Union army reached the city's outskirts after a three-month march southward from Chattanooga, Atlanta fell into chaos. Many residents prepared for the inevitable battle for the city; others fled with any possessions they could carry. Evidence of the brutality of the fighting could be seen in the increasing number of burials in the cemetery: 270 were recorded in May 1864, and 517 in June, before Sexton Pilgrim abandoned Atlanta for safer territory. Although burials continued, no records would be kept until the sexton returned in January 1865.

From positions two miles east of the city, Union artillery fired the first shells into Atlanta on the afternoon of July 20. Two days later, fierce fighting between the massed armies broke out on a line northward from Bald Hill (1-20 at Moreland Avenue) past Decatur Road. For most of the afternoon, the Battle of Atlanta raged. Sherman watched its ebb and flow from his headquarters at the home of Augustus Hurt atop nearby Copenhill (the site of the Carter Presidential Center), as depicted in the painting at the Atlanta Cyclorama in Grant Park.

The Confederate commander, General John B. Hood, observed the fighting from several locations, including the second story of the home of future Atlanta mayor James E. Williams, south of the Georgia Railroad line (today, the site is within Oakland Cemetery, near the Bell Tower). Hood, crippled by previous war injuries, had to be carried to this observation post. By day's end, the Rebels had been driven back, and the month-long siege of Atlanta began.

With the final defeat of rebel forces at Jonesboro, Georgia, on September 1, 1864, and the capture of the last railroad line, Atlanta's fate was sealed. Before evacuating the city, Rebel cavalry torched eighty-one carloads of ammunition and supplies, along with seven locomotives, parked on the Georgia Railroad tracks adjacent to the Atlanta Rolling Mill (a block east of Oakland Cemetery, near the present-day intersection of Boulevard and Decatur Street). The massive explosions scattered debris over great distances, some of it undoubtedly landing amid the cemetery's gravestones. Under smoke-filled skies on the morning of September 2, 1864, Mayor James Calhoun rode out Marietta Road under a flag of truce and surrendered the city. By noon, the Stars and Stripes flew from city hall. The next day, Sherman telegraphed Washington: "Atlanta is ours and fairly won."[8]

Over the next two months, the neglected cemetery suffered additional damage at the hands of the occupying federal troops. Fences were torn down, horses grazed among the graves, and there were reported incidents of vandalism by a few occupation troops searching tombs and crypts for hidden valuables.

As Union troops prepared to leave Atlanta in early November 1864, Sherman issued orders to burn the city's business district, including railroad depots, warehouses, and commercial buildings. According to local legend, Father Thomas O'Reilly, the pastor of a small Roman Catholic congregation, asked that Union troops spare several churches, including his own, that were in the path of this destruction. (While this endearing story has been told for nearly 150 years, present-day historians have found no confirming proof of its authenticity.) While O'Reilly is not interred at Oakland (he rests in a crypt at the nearby Shrine of the Immaculate Conception Roman Catholic Church), the Hibernian Benevolent Society donated land in the cemetery to his memory in 1873.

Atlanta Rolling Mill, destroyed during the Battle of Atlanta. Oakland Cemetery is to the right of the image.

Through the Eyes of a Child

TEN-YEAR-OLD Carrie Berry wrote of these events in her diary on September 2, 1864:

> We all woke up this morning without sleeping much last night. The Confederates had four engenes and a long train of box cars filled with ammunition and set it on fire last night which caused a grate explosion which kept us all awake.... Everyone has been trying to get all they could before the Federals come in the morning. They have been running with saques of meal, salt and tobacco. They did act rediculous breaking open stores and robbing them. About twelve o'clock there were a few Federals came in. They were all frightened. We were afraid they were going to treat us badly. It was not long before the infantry came in. They were orderly and behaved very well. I think I shall like the Yankees very well.

Union soldiers gather in Atlanta after the city's surrender.

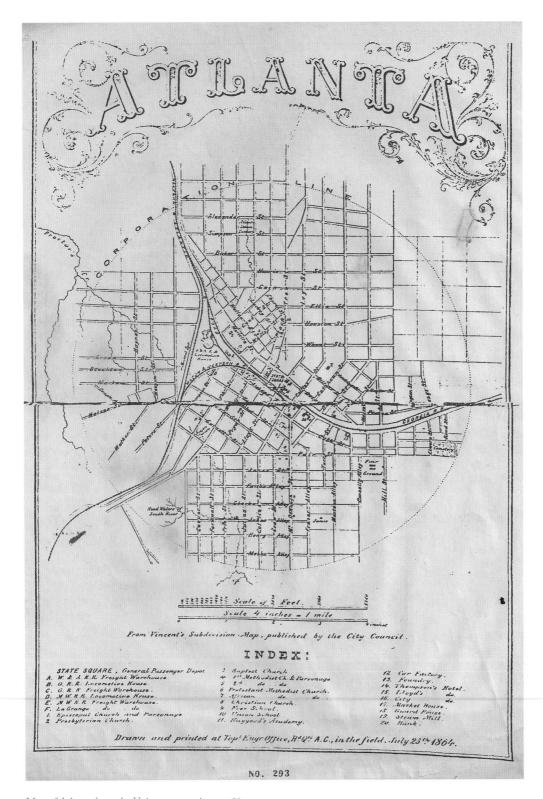

Map of Atlanta drawn by Union army engineers, 1864

Death in mid-nineteenth-century America was, for the most part, an intimate family experience. People rarely traveled far from their birthplaces, and when they died, the bodies were bathed, groomed, dressed, and laid out in the family home by loved ones until burial in a churchyard, family plot, or local cemetery. Religious traditions and burial rituals supported the prevailing Christian belief in the eventual resurrection of the physical body and a reunification with loved ones on the Day of Judgment.

The Civil War shattered these strongly held traditions: hundreds of thousands of young men were killed in combat or died from illness far from home and family. In *This Republic of Suffering*, Faust notes: "Death's significance for the Civil War generation arose as well from its violation of prevailing assumptions about life's proper end—about who should die, when, and where, and under what circumstances." She continues, "For those Americans who lived in and through the Civil War, the texture of the experience, its warp and woof, was the presence of death."[9]

Too often, civilians caught up in the conflict could not escape the war's tragic toll. Devastation wrought by battles, pestilences arising from unburied bodies, and diseases rampaging through hospitals and camps ensured that noncombatants succumbed to illnesses at a rate far above that seen before the conflict.

Especially hard hit were children, and three burial markers at Oakland poignantly tell of tragedies that befell Atlanta's civilians during the war. First is the Bloomfield family's monument, which records the tragic death of four daughters from diphtheria in a ten-day period in January 1863. Another is the small tombstone for two-year-old John Morgan Dye, who died on July 20, 1864. His mother, Sarah Dye, traveled to the cemetery later that same day to bury him while the city was under Union artillery bombardment. A third is the grave of sixteen-year-old Augusta "Gussie" King Clayton, who died of typhoid contracted while helping in a hospital during the 1864 siege. She was buried in the garden behind the family's home on Walton Street, and her remains were not moved to Oakland Cemetery for several years (see sidebar).

While these incidents took place during wartime, they also reflect the common occurrence of childhood deaths from acute illnesses such as diphtheria, consumption (tuberculosis), measles, and typhoid in the era before medical advances were available to prevent or treat them. It has been estimated that more than one-third of those buried at Oakland were children.

In early 1865, Atlanta lay in ruins. Mayor James Calhoun reported to the city council that the cemetery also was in a "deplorable condition" and that "for some five months, we had to bury the dead on credit."[10] Despite the devastation,

The Death and Burial of Augusta King Clayton

AS SHOWN IN THE FOLLOWING ACCOUNT, civilian funerals during the siege of Atlanta were haphazardly organized and often dangerous for the mourners.

[Gussie] died the following Friday, the twenty-second of July, about two o-clock, just as the battle below Oakland Cemetery was beginning. . . . As it was not at all certain to which side the victory of battle would fall, friends and neighbors, who were all kindness itself, and did everything in their power to help, advised that funeral arrangements should not be delayed. But amid the terror and demoralization throughout the town, the difficulty was in getting something done. Mr. Purse went up town to see about a casket, but could not succeed in getting it home, and Captain Lowry and his father-in-law Mr. Markham took a light wagon to the latter, drove to the undertaker and brought it to the house themselves.

Mr. Purse got the Reverend Mr. Freeman of St. Philip's Church to come

in the afternoon and officiate at the burial at which a number of friends were also in attendance, although of her sisters, only Mallie, the youngest, could be present. To think of getting to the cemetery was out of the question and there was nothing else to do but to make a place of burial in the garden and even this was dangerous for all who were there, as shells from the battlefield fell not many feet from them before the services were ended.

This was her resting place for years before a removal to the cemetery could be determined upon, and then an order to have it done as privately as possible, and to avoid the gaze of the curious, the very early morning was selected for the time; all the preparations were made at three o'clock and the different members of the family going singly, or in pairs, met at sunrise for the interment at Oakland Cemetery.

(Clayton, *Requiem for a Lost City*, 125–26)

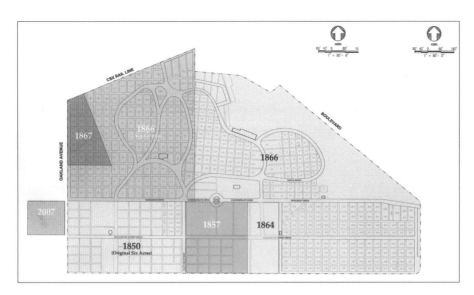

Atlanta remained the transportation hub of the South, and rebuilding began soon after hostilities ended. Within a year, the sounds of hammers and saws signaled Atlanta's rebirth (symbolized in the city's new seal, depicting the mythic phoenix rising from the ashes). The population quickly grew, and the city council allocated funds for the acquisition of additional land for the cemetery. According to cemetery records, small lowland parcels along the western boundary were acquired from A. W. Wooding and Lewis Schofield in 1866, along with 23.5 acres from Colonel Lemuel P. Grant, who owned a large tract of land south of the cemetery (a portion of which would later become Grant Park). The following year, a strip of land on the northwestern boundary was purchased from Mrs. Salina Boling. With these acquisitions, the cemetery reached its present size of approximately forty-eight acres.

Atlanta Ladies Memorial Association and Confederate Memorial Day

Throughout the war, Northern and Southern women—mothers, wives, and loved ones—bore most heavily the terrible burden of mourning. In the South, the presence of invading armies, the physical destruction of homes, and the uncertain fate of loved ones far away rendered the prevailing rituals of grief and mourning—from proper clothing to funeral details—nearly impossible to observe. Faust quotes an 1864 article from the *Daily South Carolinian* that posed the question "Who has not lost a friend during the war? We are literally a land of mourning."[11] She goes on to characterize Southern women as "a uniformed sorority of grief."

With the South's defeat in 1865, it remained for women to bear the tremendous burden of honoring the dead. Throughout the region, communities raised funds and organized Ladies Memorial Associations to carry out many tasks, including exhuming the fallen from battlefield graves, reburying them closer to home, and erecting permanent monuments to "our Confederate dead." Among the most active of these groups was the Atlanta Ladies Memorial Association (ALMA).

ALMA was founded on April 15, 1866, only three days after the first Ladies Memorial Association had been organized, in Columbus, Georgia. The association's primary purpose was to honor Confederate soldiers who had fallen in battle or died in local hospitals and had been buried in the Atlanta Cemetery. The dedicated women, many the spouses, widows, or mothers of soldiers, went to work immediately to clean the Confederate burial grounds of debris, fashion cedar wreaths to place on the graves, and plan a fitting commemoration of the dead.

Mrs. Eugenia Morgan became the first president of ALMA and tirelessly served the organization until her death, in 1924. During that first year, her husband, Major Joseph Morgan, painstakingly crafted more than five hundred wooden headboards to mark the graves and designed the layout of the Confederate section of the cemetery, a plan still in use today. The wooden headboards did not last long in the Georgia soil, and most had been replaced with more durable marble markers by 1900.

On April 29, 1866, Atlanta's first Confederate Memorial Day ceremonies were held on the cemetery grounds. Local businesses closed for the morning, and as a witness later recalled, "The people young and old were seen wending their way to the cemetery, most of them bearing some floral tribute to be deposited above the silent dust of the Confederate soldiers. The city of the living was deserted, for the time, for the city of the dead."[12]

The following year, the Confederate Memorial Day commemoration was held on April 26, the anniversary of the 1865 surrender of Confederate general Joseph E. Johnston's army to General Sherman's forces in North Carolina, a date marked by many as the end of the war. Georgia became the first southern state to declare this a legal holiday, and it remains so today (the annual commemoration ceremony is held on the Saturday nearest the anniversary).

In the first few years after the war, the federal government appropriated funds to establish national cemeteries for the reinterment of Union battlefield dead, but the devastated South had scant resources, except private generosity, for such a massive undertaking. Among ALMA's stated goals was to raise the necessary funds to locate and exhume the bodies of Confederate soldiers, many unidentified and buried in hastily dug battlefield graves around Atlanta, for the purpose of "giving these neglected heroes a Christian burial."[13] For many of these women, the fallen soldiers they so faithfully found, carefully exhumed, and lovingly reburied in the Atlanta Cemetery served as proxies for their own kin tragically lost and buried far from home.

In 1867, ALMA petitioned the Atlanta City Council for a parcel of land in the cemetery for the interment of the unknown dead. The council honored this request, assigning tracts in sections H, I, J, and K and in an area north of K for the placement of the unknowns. In 1868, Mrs. Fannie Gordon, the wife of General John B. Gordon, who served under General Robert E. Lee in Virginia and later as governor of Georgia, was elected the second president of ALMA. Through her tireless efforts, enough money was raised to begin the work of locating and reinterring the Confederate dead from battlefield graves. The task was completed early the following year.

Following the 1869 Confederate Memorial Day ceremonies, ALMA led an effort to erect a suitable monument to honor the fallen. More than $1,200 was raised, but there was disagreement on the proper location for the memorial. Mrs. Gordon and several other members supported its placement in the heart of the city at Five Points; many others believed it should be located in the Confederate section of the cemetery, nearly a mile from the town center. The cemetery site was ultimately chosen, and Mrs. Gordon resigned as ALMA's president over the choice. This decision served to make Oakland the focal point for nearly all Confederate Memorial Day events as well as an important destination for visitors to Atlanta. Mrs. Mary Willis Cobb Johnson, a sister of the Confederate generals Howell Cobb and T. R. R. Cobb, succeeded Fannie Gordon and, after the 1870 Confederate Memorial Day program, completed the necessary fund-raising to lay the monument's cornerstone in the center of the Confederate Memorial Grounds.

At a somber ceremony on October 15, 1870, the same day as General Robert E. Lee's funeral in Lexington, Virginia, a small space at the monument's base was filled with artifacts and sealed with mortar. Franklin Garrett described this event in *Atlanta and Environs*: "A large assemblage then moved out Hunter Street to the cemetery where appropriate ceremonies were held in conjunction with the laying of the cornerstone of the Confederate Monument. A Confederate flag was deposited inside, while a bottle of wine, kept since 1861, was poured over the stone. Eloquent addresses were made by Grand Master Samuel Lawrence, of the Masons, and by Colonel Thomas C. Howard."[14]

Fund-raising for the monument was successful, and the sixty-five-foot-high obelisk, constructed of Stone Mountain granite and inscribed with a shield bearing the words "Our Confederate Dead—1873," was completed in January 1874. It was unveiled before an audience of nearly fifteen thousand at the Confederate Memorial Day commemoration that April. At the time of its dedication, the monument rivaled the Kimball House Hotel (ca. 1870) as the tallest structure in the city. More than a century later, it has been dwarfed by the Atlanta skyline, but remains the centerpiece of the cemetery.

Postcard of the Confederate Monument and Fort Walker, early twentieth century

Nearly ten years later, the Atlanta Ladies Memorial Association requested permission from the city council to sell some of the unused land it had been given for burial of unknown soldiers. The interments had been completed, and ALMA hoped to raise additional funds for the erection of two marble shafts in the Confederate section to be inscribed with the names of the soldiers buried at Oakland without identifying headstones.

The women of ALMA took great pride in their efforts at memorialization. On April 26, 1890, ALMA's treasurer, Mrs. George Fry, proclaimed in a Confederate Memorial Day speech that women of the association had "worked with untiring energy, until they had built a monument . . . and paid for the stones that marked their soldiers' graves."[15]

In 1891, the mayor and city council finally approved the request, and within a short time, all the lots were sold. Some of the choicest tracts were purchased by ALMA's leaders for their own families, while another large parcel was sold to the Hebrew Benevolent Congregation for $2,000. A short time later, this parcel was subdivided and a portion resold to the newly established Ahavath Achim Congregation, composed largely of Russian, Polish, and eastern European immigrants.

In addition to the funds raised for the two marble shafts, ALMA raised money to commission the Georgia sculptor T. M. Brady (later the mayor of Canton, Georgia) to carve a suitable memorial to be placed in the center of the Confederate Memorial Grounds, where the bodies of three thousand unknown soldiers were interred. Brady created a monument depicting a dying lion grasping a Confederate battle flag. The massive statue, believed to be the largest ever carved from a single block of Georgia marble, resembled the renowned *Lion of Lucerne* (1820–21), located in Switzerland, which honors the Swiss Guards massacred in defense of the French royal family during the French Revolution. After more than a year of painstaking work, the powerful and poignant monument, known as the *Lion of Atlanta*, was unveiled to admiring crowds on Confederate Memorial Day 1894.

In a touching sidebar to this story, Atlanta suffered a late-spring cold snap that killed most of the flowers needed for this Confederate Memorial Day commemoration. The residents of Brunswick, Georgia, remembering the support given to them by Atlantans when their city was devastated by a yellow fever epidemic in 1893, collected and shipped to Atlanta a railway car full of fresh-cut flowers to grace the soldiers' graves.

Postcard of the *Lion of Atlanta* sculpture, early twentieth century

In the aftermath of the Civil War, the federal government had paid for headstones for the Union dead. Recognizing the work done by organizations like ALMA and wanting to promote regional reconciliation, President William McKinley spoke at the Georgia Capitol in 1898. Himself a Union army veteran, McKinley sought to unite all who mourned the war's terrible losses, proclaiming to his audience, "What an array of silent sentinels we have, and with what loving care their graves are kept! Every soldier's grave made during our unfortunate civil war is a tribute to American valor. . . . The time has now come in the evolution of sentiment and feeling under the providence of God, when in the spirit of fraternity we should share with you in care of the graves of Confederate soldiers."[16] Heeding McKinley's call, within a decade Congress appropriated funds to erect markers to the Confederate dead interred in northern cemeteries.

A Rural Sculpture Garden Park Called Oakland

America's early rural garden cemeteries, notably Mount Auburn (1831) outside Boston, Greenwood (1838) in Brooklyn, and Laurel Hill (1836) in Philadelphia, were developed by private companies and marketed to wealthy families. Their design reflected the evolving view of cemeteries as tastefully laid-out and carefully tended pastoral landscapes of remembrance. In *Rural Essays* (1853), the pioneering landscape designer Andrew Jackson Downing wrote: "One of the most remarkable illustrations of the popular taste, in this country, is to be found in the rise and progress of our rural cemeteries."[17]

Unlike these outstanding examples of the rural garden cemetery movement, Oakland began as a public burial ground that evolved somewhat haphazardly as the city grew. It was not until the decades following the Civil War, as Atlanta

rebuilt and prospered, that the grounds began to truly resemble a rural garden cemetery.

Four years after the Civil War ended, as ALMA was raising funds for the Confederate Memorial, work was taking place elsewhere in the cemetery. The grounds were again enclosed by a fence, a night watchman was employed to protect the public and private property, and Sexton Green Pilgrim resigned, to be succeeded by John Connolly. Under Connolly's supervision, plans were drawn up for the construction of a building to house the sexton's office and a small chapel.

Atlanta's renaissance attracted entrepreneurs and visionaries hoping to make their fortunes. Men like Marion Kiser, Robert Richards, Alfred Austell, and others started new businesses, constructed retail and manufacturing buildings, and built elegant residences along Peachtree and other fashionable streets. They purchased lots in the Atlanta Cemetery, improving them with flowers and greenery. In time, they also erected elaborate mausoleums and monuments rich in funerary symbolism, reflecting the Victorians' romantic interest in Greek, Roman, Gothic, and Eclectic design, as well as their own elevated station in life. The historian Diana Williams Combs noted, "Victorians in their rural cemeteries wished to create legacies of imperishable mortal wealth. . . . It was thought necessary to maintain the standards of one's class in death as in life, and if possible, even to use death as a means of further social advancement."[18]

In 1872, recognizing the ongoing transformation of the grounds, Sexton Connolly petitioned the city council for funds to construct a small structure in the cemetery to protect plants during winter. This is believed to have been among the first greenhouses erected in Atlanta. At year's end, the Cemetery Committee submitted to the council a proposal to give the property a more pleasing name, suggesting that, henceforth, the cemetery should be called "Oakland," in reference to the abundance of oak trees within the grounds and their significance as symbols of strength, longevity, and protection. The change of name also reflected the evolution of the site from a utilitarian burial ground into a garden park for the enjoyment of the living.

Great value was also placed on the continued transformation of Oakland into a coherent landscape based on rustic simplicity and contentment. As noted by Noble Calhoun Williams in *Echoes from the Battlefield; or, Southern Life during the War* (1902): "Oakland Cemetery, situated on an eminence which overlooks the city to the westward and the beautiful farming country for miles around to the south and east, is picturesquely beautiful with its trees and shrubbery, lawns, flowers, driveways, vaults, and marble shafts."[19]

Atlanta skyline as seen from Oakland, 1870s

In a city with few public parks, Oakland became an increasingly popular destination for residents, who enjoyed strolling about the grounds, relaxing on benches, or enjoying picnics among the monuments. The Historic Oakland Foundation's annual "Sunday in the Park" re-creates this nineteenth-century tradition.

A Place Apart

As the cemetery acquired additional land to the north and east, Slave Square became coveted space near the heart of the burial ground. With interment space at a premium in postwar Atlanta, white residents called for the relocation of slaves' bodies to the recently extended eastern boundaries of the cemetery so that the space could be reused for white burials. To accommodate this demand, the city council issued the following resolution in 1877: "Resolved that the City Sexton be hereby authorized and instructed to remove the bodies from what is called slave square, in that portion of the old cemetery west of the Confederate Grounds, and that the square be leveled and divided into lots of suitable size, and that said lots be sold for no less than $50.00 each, and that the bones or bodies removed from said lots be reinterred in the colored pauper grounds without any distinction of graves, except those who may have headboards, who may be interred by themselves."[20] While such actions offend our modern sensibilities, they serve as a painful yet inescapable reminder of the low social status, near powerlessness, and marginal existence of Atlanta's black residents during the era of slavery and the nearly century-long period of segregation that followed.

As these remains were being relocated, Atlanta's growing African American working- and middle-class residents sought a section within the cemetery where they could properly bury their dead. Space had been previously set aside near the paupers' area for black interments, and this was adequate for a few years, but by the late 1870s, the area was reaching capacity, with little additional space available for future burials.

Beginning in February 1878, Atlanta's black business and community leaders made several requests to the city council for more space at Oakland. The issue was referred to the Cemetery Committee, but no action was taken. A short time later, black leaders petitioned for a separate cemetery. The committee agreed, but again failed to allocate any funds for land. For several years, this issue lay dormant while the spaces available for both white and black burials at Oakland continued to diminish.

In his 1882 "Annual Report," Mayor James English noted that Oakland was now surrounded by development on all sides, making further expansion

Map of Atlanta showing Oakland Cemetery, 1877

expensive, maybe even impossible. He wrote, "It is now quite evident that it [Oakland] must be enlarged at an early day or a new cemetery established elsewhere. All the more desirable lots have been purchased, and persons now desiring to purchase lots find it impossible to get them desirably located."[21]

The mayor closed with an urgent plea for legislative action that would grant the city the authority to condemn land for cemetery purposes, but local landowners were successful in halting this proposal. On May 5, 1884, the city council and the board of aldermen agreed to support the development of a new, privately owned and operated cemetery west of Atlanta. This new facility, called Westview, opened for white interments, including pauper burials, later that year.

At the same time, black leaders renewed their petition for a separate burial ground. This time, it was granted, and land was acquired south of the city on Jonesboro Road. The new burial ground, called South-View, opened in 1886 and fulfilled the burial needs of subsequent generations of black Atlantans. Two years later, the city council finalized a contract with South-View for the future burial of black paupers.

Fulton Bag and Cotton Mill as seen from Oakland, 1880s

Even with the opening of the new cemetery, a number of Atlanta's pioneering black residents were interred in Oakland's "colored section" well into the twentieth century. Among them were the ex-slave Carrie Steele Logan (d. 1900), the founder of an orphanage for black children; Roderick Badger (d. 1890), who learned dentistry from his white master (who was also his father) and went on to become the city's first black dentist; Bishop Wesley John Gaines (d. 1912), the second pastor of Big Bethel African Methodist Episcopal Church and a founder of Morris Brown College; Henry Butler, MD (d. 1931), and his wife, the educator Selena Sloan Butler (d. 1964); and the real estate developer Antoine Graves (d. 1941), who erected the only mausoleum in Oakland's African American section.

In 1896, the Boylston family was given permission to bury their former slave and servant, Catherine Holmes, in the family's lot, located, ironically, in the area of the old Slave Square. She was the only African American interred in the white area of the cemetery until 1920, when the Boyd family was granted permission from Mayor James L. Key (who had gotten the approval of adjoining lot owners) to bury their longtime servant, Georgia Harris, in the family's plot. Poignantly, Harris's tombstone proclaimed that she, "Who—though born a slave died the child of a King."

Grave of Georgia Harris

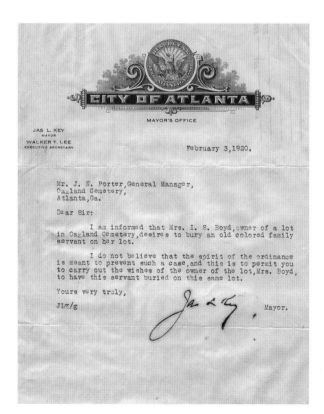

Mayor James Key's letter regarding the burial of Georgia Harris, February 3, 1920

The Most Attractive Place in the City

Even as burial lots were being purchased at Westview, improvements at Oakland continued unabated. During the later years of the nineteenth century and the early years of the twentieth, Oakland continued to evolve into an exceptional example of a rural garden cemetery, often described as a "heaven on earth" for the dearly departed. A mix of lush landscaping, profuse flowers, footpaths, meandering carriageways, and ornately carved markers and elegant monuments contributed to what Mayor George Hillyer described as "the most attractive place in the city where decorous and orderly throngs of our citizens congregate every pleasant Sunday to quietly pass through the well kept grounds."[22]

To support and enhance the lush grounds, water and sewer lines were extended to Oakland, and the walks and drives were lined with bricks. In 1892, public lot sales were reopened, and the proceeds were used to extend a rock wall along Fair Street to Boulevard. The following year, two comfort stations for white patrons were erected to meet visitors' needs. The new sexton, T. A. Clayton, urged the city to provide an annual appropriation for the upkeep and beautification of Oakland in order that it might be regarded as "the prettiest cemetery in the South."[23]

In 1894, the major roads within the grounds were bordered with stone, gutters were laid, and landscaping was done in the public areas. To enhance security, cemetery employees were issued uniforms with badges and granted police powers within the property's boundaries.

Anticipating increased visitation to Oakland during the Cotton States and International Exposition, to be held in Atlanta in 1895, Clayton secured funds for additional improvements. These included the erection of a brick wall enclosing the cemetery with formal gateways on Hunter Street (now Martin Luther King Jr. Drive) and Fair Street (now Memorial Drive). Despite these achievements, Clayton was forced to resign after being suspected of "irregularities" in cemetery operations; he was succeeded by Clarence Stephens, a nephew of Alexander Stephens, the former congressman, Confederate vice president, and governor. The new sexton oversaw the completion of these projects, but died in 1898; he was buried at Oakland.

In 1899, an elaborate new cemetery office designed in the Gothic Revival style was built at a cost of $4,600. The facility, located on the

Oakland Cemetery's Hunter Street entrance gate, ca. 1900

site of the original sexton's building, featured a cemetery office, receiving vaults, waiting rooms, and a second-floor residence for the sexton's family. A new greenhouse and other maintenance facilities were completed the same year. In 1901, a small brick watchhouse was erected at the Hunter Street Gate to serve as both a visitor center and a security checkpoint.

Oakland Cemetery's greenhouse, 1960s

The dawn of a new century ushered in an era of change at Oakland. Following the 1907 creation of a new Cemetery Commission composed of the mayor, the cemetery committee chair, and five elected lot owners, the cemetery underwent notable improvements. Shortly before World War I, the long-overdue paving of Hunter Street was completed to the cemetery entrance, and more interior lanes were paved. A book of cemetery rules and regulations was published, and cemetery staffing (security, grounds, and maintenance workers) reached its zenith in 1914.

Even as these positive changes were being implemented, undercurrents that would have long-term consequences for the operation of the cemetery were at work. The former Oakland Cemetery librarian Kent Moore writes of this period: "Oakland was becoming a persistent thorn in the [City] Council's side, and the new Commission obviously viewed the site, which had been assembled piecemeal, to be antiquated and hopelessly inadequate for a city of Atlanta's stature."[24]

Political disagreements among the commission, the Cemetery Committee, and the city council continually hindered operations. In 1907, the commission abolished the sexton's position (in part out of dislike of the incumbent, H. H. Barefield), replacing it with a lower-salaried superintendent and a registrar to manage accounts. Four years later, against the wishes of the commission, the Cemetery Committee eliminated the superintendent's job, causing members of the commission to threaten resignation. Despite these tensions, the registrar, John Porter, accepted a new role as Oakland's general manager—at least until 1914, when Mayor James Woodward tried to cut the manager's salary, arguing that it did not constitute a full-time job.

Undoubtedly, effective management of Oakland was complicated by many factors. Notable among them were incomplete or conflicting records of ownership for many private lots, with some disputes going back more than a half century; a lack of control over private contractors working in the cemetery; few provisions for, and little funding of, the perpetual care of private lots; and insufficient funds for the maintenance and repair of monuments and markers, especially those for which there was no longer any private support.

During this time, the city once again made changes to the racial ordering of the cemetery. Driven by the demand for additional places for white interments, the commission ordered the removal of all black pauper bodies located south of Confederate Drive. This was done, and the remains relocated to Potters' Field. The lots were resold to white families awaiting access to burial space. Although African Americans buried in Potters' Field had no grave markers, those buried in the colored section set aside for paid burials had memorials. The commissioners noted the improvements, reporting that the section "now represents a decent appearance to the gratification of the better class of Negroes who are taking an interest in the cemetery for the first time, and are expressing a desire to beautify their ground."[25]

The Confederate Memorial Day celebrations held on April 26, 1918, as thousands of American doughboys were fighting in France, marked a final salute to the dwindling number of Confederate veterans who marched in the parade to the cemetery. The *Atlanta Journal* captured the spirit of the day: "Under gray skies they marched, but with heads held proudly high and banners fluttering—the Stars and Bars and the Stars and Stripes—while from every side rose cheers and handclapping in honor of the men who gave their all for Dixie in 1861 and the men who are giving their all for America today."[26] While most of these old soldiers would soon be gone, the last recorded interment at Oakland of a Confederate veteran took place on February 11, 1937, with the burial, in section E, row 1 of the Confederate Memorial Grounds, of G. A. Seymour of the Forty-Sixth Georgia Infantry Regiment, Army of Tennessee.

Following World War I, political disagreements and financial problems continued to plague Oakland, leading to the abolition of the Cemetery Commission in 1921. A growing number of private lots and grave sites were abandoned by families or long-lost deed holders, placing an increasing burden on the cemetery's meager staff to keep them from becoming choked with weeds and debris.

Interments at Oakland continued to decline because of its diminishing capacity and the growing popularity of Westview and South-View as well as the establishment in 1904 of Greenwood Cemetery, with its large Jewish burial ground. Nonetheless, many prominent Atlantans with family ties to the cemetery were laid to rest at Oakland throughout the twentieth and early twenty-first centuries. Among them were Joseph Jacobs, a pharmacist (d. 1925); Joel Hurt, a real estate developer (d. 1926); Jacob Elsas, the owner of the Fulton Bag and Cotton Mill (d. 1932); former governor Joseph M. Brown (d. 1932); the author Margaret Mitchell Marsh (d. 1949); former governor John M. Slaton (d. 1955); the golfer and attorney Robert Tyre "Bobby" Jones Jr. (d. 1971); the historian Franklin Garrett (d. 2000); and former mayors Maynard Jackson (d. 2003) and Ivan Allen Jr. (d. 2003, reinterred at Oakland in 2009).

As the Great Depression descended over Atlanta and the nation, Oakland suffered further neglect. In 1932, the Cemetery Committee, which had been charged with oversight of the cemetery since the abolition of the cemetery commission, was itself dissolved by the city council. The property fell under the jurisdiction of the city's Parks Department, which was already suffering from dramatic cuts in budgets for basic maintenance and upkeep, not to mention operations and record keeping.

Four years later, in 1936, the Works Progress Administration (WPA), a federal agency created to provide employment to thousands of skilled workers, undertook to survey and map the cemetery and to document burial records. Writing in the *Atlanta Journal* for July 11, 1937, reporter William Neal noted the challenges facing these workers: "The thirteen men provided by the WPA, are searching for complete data on every person buried in the cemetery. . . . When the survey started nobody knew much about Oakland except what they could see as they walked through the carriage drives and read the tombstones. Records from 1850 to 1870 consist merely of the names of the persons buried and their age, the date, and cause of death. No effort was made to describe where they were buried."[27] This project, part of a nationwide effort to research and preserve burial records in hundreds of cemeteries, was the most comprehensive ever undertaken at Oakland, and the detailed maps and records created by the WPA remain a valuable resource for cemetery staff, families, genealogists, and researchers.

With the outbreak of World War II, Oakland's appearance underwent dramatic change when much of the ornamental ironwork surrounding family plots and squares was removed for use in the war effort. Today, only scattered vestiges of the once-abundant wrought iron remain. Also at this time, a mystery unfolded: the bronze doors from the mausoleum of Dr. H. H. Green, erected in 1894, disappeared. An investigation revealed that the doors had been stolen, probably for sale as scrap metal for the war. Recognizing that time was of the essence, Dr. Green's granddaughters searched local junkyards and found the doors—remarkably, undamaged. They were returned to the family's crypt and, in an effort to disguise their true materials, painted black. On the family's instruction, they remain painted to this day.

A Little Help from Its Friends

By the 1970s, Oakland was in a poor and neglected condition. But with the approach of the nation's bicentennial celebration in 1976, the cemetery's fortunes began to improve. In 1975, the Atlanta Bicentennial Commission endorsed much-needed restoration projects at Oakland. At the same time, recognizing its significance in local, state, and national history, the Georgia National Register Advisory Commission successfully nominated Oakland for placement on the National Register of Historic Places (the second cemetery in Georgia to be so honored). In an article published in the *Atlanta Constitution*, the Atlanta Parks and Recreation director, Ted Mastroianni, expressed the

Franklin M. Garrett, Atlanta's "Official Historian"

BEGINNING IN 1933, a young man often rode out to Oakland on his bicycle after completing work on the night shift at Western Union. Deeply interested in local history, Franklin M. Garrett passed hours in the cemetery transcribing the inscriptions on every marker for a planned necrology of Fulton and DeKalb Counties.

He later spent his career with the Coca-Cola Company, using his spare time to write *Atlanta and Environs: A Chronicle of Her People and Events* (2 vols., 1954). He joined the Atlanta Historical Society (now the Atlanta History Center) in 1927 and, after retiring from Coca-Cola in 1974, served for many years as president of the center, earning the

Franklin Garrett reading to children at Oakland, 1991

sobriquet the "official historian" of Atlanta. Never tiring of tramping through cemeteries, he was still at work on his necrology when he died, in 2000. Much of the information he gathered is now available through the online genealogy database of the Atlanta History Center's Kenan Research Center (www.atlantahistorycenter.com). Garrett and his wife Frances, who died in 2005, are interred together at Oakland near the Watch House.

hope that with this increased visibility, "Atlanta residents will become interested in the cemetery as a place to stroll, relax, or even picnic. It's a cemetery . . . but it's also a park."[28]

Beginning in 1974, a small group of interested Atlantans calling themselves Friends of Oakland Cemetery . . . Us started an informal organization to support and promote Oakland. As interest grew, the group, joined by others, established the nonprofit Historic Oakland Cemetery, Inc. (HOCI) in June 1976. Composed of devoted volunteers, civic and business leaders, preservationists, and descendants' families, in collaboration with the City of Atlanta and the sexton's office, the group dedicated itself to preserving, restoring, and interpreting the historic cemetery for present and future generations. Through donations and grants from the Parks Department, HOCI also took a lead role in stabilizing and restoring walks, interior walls, and several cemetery structures. At the same time, it undertook campaigns to increase Oakland's financial resources in order to ensure the cemetery's future as an integral part of Atlanta's history. In this effort, the group was aided by members of the Atlanta Junior League, who conducted cemetery tours and carried Oakland's story to numerous organizations across the city.

In the ensuing four decades, the organization (the name was changed to the Historic Oakland Foundation in 1996), working closely with the city as well as with other individuals and groups, has undertaken several major initiatives to stabilize the grounds and structures, begin their restoration, and improve understanding and documentation of the cemetery's historical significance. In 1978, the foundation commissioned a cultural resources survey of Potters' Field. Careful excavation revealed that several thousand people had been interred in the open meadow. While nearly all were black, a significant number had not been paupers, based on the quality of the caskets and objects uncovered. These findings changed the long-held perception that the field had been simply a place for disposing of the bodies of those without means.

The following year, students studying the building trades at Atlanta Area Technical College, working under the close supervision of instructors and with funds provided by the City of Atlanta, carried out extensive restorations and repairs of brick retaining walls throughout the cemetery. A third initiative was the careful restoration, beginning in 1994, of the Confederate Memorial Grounds, undertaken by volunteers from the Alfred Holt Colquitt Chapter of the United Daughters of the Confederacy and the Sons of Confederate Veterans. This extensive project was chronicled in the book *Headstones of Heroes: The Restoration and History of Confederate Graves in Atlanta's Oakland Cemetery*, by Robert Zaworski.

A community project in 2005 involved the transplanting of plants and shrubbery from the soon-to-be-demolished Grady Homes public housing complex near Oakland. With the help of volunteers, dozens of plants, including camellias, hydrangeas, and azaleas, were used to beautify the cemetery's African American Grounds. A fifth project was the foundation's 2006 restoration of the Old Jewish Burial Grounds (part of the Original Six Acres), made possible by the support of Atlanta's Jewish community. Through this painstaking work, the space was carefully returned to its original appearance.

Today, Oakland remains both a city park and an active cemetery (with about a dozen interments each year). The sexton employs a small staff to handle park maintenance and burial arrangements. The foundation works closely with the sexton and with the Department of Parks, Recreation and Cultural Affairs, as well as the Atlanta Urban Design Commission, to plan and oversee landscape-beautification projects, care for private lots, and repair damaged or toppled tombstones and monuments.

To meet these responsibilities, the foundation staff and dozens of dedicated volunteers carry out myriad tasks, including staffing the visitors center, participating in landscaping projects, and leading guided tours, which range from the popular "Sights, Symbols, and Stories" overview tour to an ever-changing variety of themed tours exploring the cemetery's links to the Civil War, pioneer Atlanta, funerary symbolism, and the area's African American heritage. School groups from around the Southeast visit Oakland to discover its significance in the history of Atlanta and Georgia.

Oakland guide Al Stephens leading a Civil War tour, 2010

The foundation sponsors several signature events during the year. Especially popular are "Sunday in the Park," for which attendees are encouraged to wear Victorian-era clothing; "Capturing the Spirit of Oakland" Halloween candlelight tours, which fill a weekend before Halloween; the annual "Run Like Hell" 5K footrace (and the "Run Like Heck" 1K fun run); and the "Tunes from the Tombs" music festival. Given its popularity as one of Atlanta's most historic and unique green spaces, Oakland has become a favorite destination for weddings, birthday parties, corporate events, photography and art workshops, special occasions, and, of course, the occasional funeral.

Resurgens

When rebuilding from the Civil War's devastation, Atlanta adopted a new city seal, one depicting the mythic phoenix rising from the ashes and the motto "Resurgens" ("rising again"). Following the events on the night of March 14, 2008, the same could apply to Oakland Cemetery. About ten thirty at night, as a basketball tournament was underway at the nearby Georgia Dome, a powerful tornado struck downtown Atlanta, causing millions of dollars of damage and one fatality. A number of small buildings were destroyed, and the Georgia World Congress Center, the Westin Peachtree Plaza Hotel, and several other high-rise structures suffered significant damage. But the destruction at Oakland Cemetery may have been the most devastating.

Sexton Sam Reed, along with a security officer, weathered the storm by huddling in the Bell Tower. The sound of wind and rain was punctuated by the gunshot-like cracks of century-old trees being snapped and ornate monuments being demolished. Robbie Brown described the scene for the *New York Times*: "Even proud old Oakland was no match for the tornado that battered downtown Atlanta. . . . At the cemetery, trees were crushed, stone angels that guarded family memorials were decapitated, and gravestones planted even before Sherman burned the city were toppled."[29] Once the storm subsided, Reed ventured outside to witness a scene he could have never imagined.

The immediate need was clear—to request a Federal Emergency Management Agency (FEMA) assessment and begin the removal of trees and limbs that blocked roads and threatened to do further damage to fragile structures. Work on these tasks began soon after with the aid of prisoners provided by the State Department of Corrections. Next was an assessment of what had to be done to stabilize endangered and damaged structures and to begin the slow but critical effort of repairing and restoring the hallowed ground.

In an interview with the *Atlanta Journal-Constitution*, Kevin Kuharic noted that strict preservation guidelines governed much of the painstaking work. He pointed out that a ninety-day moratorium was placed on repair work so that "each root ball" could be "inspected by archeologists to make sure it had no artifacts." He added, "When we do something, we have confidence we're handling it in a sensitive and appropriate way."[30] Over many months, and with the support of the City of Atlanta, the Georgia Emergency Management Agency, FEMA, and countless organizations and tireless volunteers, Oakland slowly arose, like the mythic phoenix, from the devastation. Because of the difficult and often dangerous process of debris removal, repair, and restoration work, Oakland was closed to the public for three months, reopening in the summer of 2008. Thousands of visitors flocked to see the

Downed trees from a severe tornado, March 2008

historic ground, many with a renewed appreciation for a landscape they may have overlooked.

Among the most significant and symbolic repairs was the restoration of the soaring monument on the family lot of Governor Joseph E. Brown (the Civil War governor of Georgia) and his son, Governor Joseph M. Brown. Erected in 1873, the tall shaft topped by a seven-foot statue of the archangel Gabriel had been shattered by the force of the tornado, and many experts believed that the monument was beyond repair. Through the efforts of the foundation staff, the preservation studio at the Atlanta architectural firm of Lord, Aeck and Sargent, the talents of Chris Phillips (a Savannah mason), and many others, the badly damaged statue and its supporting base were returned to their honored place at Oakland only seven months after the tornado struck. On the day the crane lifted Gabriel into place, Kuharic noted: "The monuments are really symbols of recovery. We deliberately chose to start with major monuments to set the tone for the rest of the effort."[31]

In the years since the tornado struck, historic Oakland Cemetery has continued to undergo a restoration renaissance. Atlantans are rediscovering the simple pleasure of a stroll around the grounds, and visitors from across the world now include a tour of Oakland as an essential part of their sojourn in Atlanta. While the first 160 years were filled with challenge, the outlook for Oakland's future looks bright.

Two

Historic Oakland and the Elements of the Rural Garden Cemetery Movement

Oakland Cemetery was founded in the wake of a marked change in prevailing attitudes toward death, burial, and commemoration of the dead.

DIANA COMBS, *Atlanta Historical Bulletin*, 1976

FOR CENTURIES, burial grounds were little more than rough patches of earth where dead bodies were often haphazardly disposed of in order to deal with the foul odors of decay and the risk of disease. Few people had the resources to inscribe markers for the departed, and fewer still the ability to read them. With the erection of churches in towns and countryside, parishioners sought to be interred in their church's burial ground, often called "God's acre," or, if their station in the community warranted, within the sanctuary itself. These grounds were usually too small and inadequate to meet the needs of large or long-standing congregations. Public burial grounds provided alternatives, but these tended to be poorly planned, neglected properties with little attraction for the living. As cities became increasingly congested, public cemeteries frequently became inadequate to meet the growing need for burials.

By 1800, the concept of the burial ground as a place to be feared and avoided began to change. The English Romantics and their nature-loving followers began to think of burial grounds as planned "parks" composed of lawns, shade trees, lush landscaping, and meandering paths—picturesque places for quiet strolls and contemplation at some distance from crowded cities or towns. They popularized the word "cemetery," from the Greek word for "sleeping chamber," to describe these spaces. Scholars point to Père Lachaise Cemetery in Paris, established in 1804, as the model for what would become a movement to create rural garden cemeteries across western Europe and, eventually, North America.

Possibly the most influential people in the development of rural garden cemeteries were the Scots landscape designer Robert Claudius Loudon and his American counterpart Andrew Jackson Downing. In 1843, shortly before his death, Loudon published *On the Laying Out, Planting, and Managing of Cemeteries, and on the Improvement of Churchyards*, which detailed his experience and views. In her book *The Victorian Cemetery*, Sarah Rutherford summed up Loudon's philosophy on the role of cemeteries in their communities: "For Loudon garden cemeteries were not merely repositories for the dead. They were far more than that, being instructive, improving of manners, morals, and taste, educational and soothing places for the resort of relatives." She continued:

"[A cemetery] might become a school of instruction in architecture, sculpture, landscape-gardening, arboriculture, botany and in those important parts of general gardening, neatness, order and high keeping, as well as serving as historical records for local history and biography."[1]

Downing, in his 1853 book *Rural Essays*, echoed this view by noting of Mount Auburn Cemetery that it "was tastefully laid out, monuments were built, and the whole highly embellished." This style of cemetery design struck a nerve, he added: "No sooner was attention generally roused to the charms of this first American cemetery, than the idea took the public mind by storm."[2]

While initial development of Atlanta's municipal burial ground was utilitarian, as the city grew and the burial ground expanded, the influence of the rural garden cemetery movement became increasingly evident. Oakland evolved into a soothing landscape suited for both the departed and those left behind. Today, Oakland represents a blend of several widely recognized rural garden cemetery styles:

GARDENESQUE. A style in which displays of a variety of plants are instantly recognizable as the work of human hands. The design often involves the use of nonnative plants and terracing. Over time, Oakland's gardenesque spaces developed into woodland gardens marked by particular use of rhododendrons, azaleas, boxwoods, camellias, and magnolias. Today, many original plantings have been systematically removed by families to create more burial spaces or by the City of Atlanta to minimize maintenance.

Thyme and dusty miller flowers in front of the Winship mausoleum, Bell Tower Ridge

Lantana flowers near the English monument, Bell Tower Ridge

Bench in the South Public Grounds

Tulips in bloom in the North Public Grounds

PICTURESQUE. Most often evocative of rural settings, these areas feature informal groupings of plants in a rolling terrain with the intention of reflecting an idealized and sentimentalized view of nature. Examples of this style may be found within some of Oakland's private burial lots, the Confederate Memorial Grounds, and the Public Grounds.

MODERNE. A twentieth-century style featuring streamlined and uncluttered space. It is found in only a single private lot.

PASTORAL. Especially notable in open, meadow-like Potters' Field, where visitors may glimpse the vestige of a rural landscape.

Winburn monument, Greenhouse Valley, the only Moderne structure at Oakland

Bench overlooking the rolling landscape of Potters' Field

Funerary Art and Architecture

What most often captures the interest of visitors to Oakland Cemetery are the abundant examples of nineteenth-century funerary art and architecture. Like its counterparts in other cities, Oakland includes wooded hills and lawns that provide space where Atlantans, rich and poor, could express themselves through the erection of markers, monuments, and memorials reflecting the designs most popular during their lifetimes.

Oakland's forty-eight acres feature an impressive array of limestone, granite, and marble art and structures in Greek Revival, Classical Revival, Gothic Revival, Egyptian Revival, and Exotic Revival styles. Works include the massive *Lion of Atlanta* in the Confederate Memorial Grounds; sculpted figures, in poses from triumphant to pensive; a wealth of religious icons, botanical images, and secular symbols; and the Gothic Revival tower where the bell still tolls for a dozen or more funerals each year.

Especially notable is the wealth of mausoleums, each representing expressions of familiar Classic designs or Eclectic styles. More than five dozen vaults and mausoleums, from simple brick or stone structures to soaring cathedrals in miniature, punctuate Oakland's landscape. Each served to define the inhabitants' prominent place in their own minds as well as in the community's social order. Several of the most elegant structures feature handcrafted stained-glass windows; the Marsh family mausoleum is noted for its two bronze urns cast at New York's Gorham Foundry, the country's first art foundry.

Opposite: Angel atop the Dougherty monument, Original Six Acres

Left: Stained-glass window in the Sage mausoleum, Bell Tower Ridge

Right: Stained-glass window in the Sanders Hickey mausoleum, Bell Tower Ridge

Origins of the Mausoleum

A MAUSOLEUM is a freestanding building constructed as a monument and burial chamber. The term is drawn from the burial structure of King Mausolus, a governor of Caria (in present-day Turkey), who died in 353 BCE. His massive tomb at Halicarnassus (near Bodrum, Turkey) stood nearly 150 feet tall and was one of the Seven Wonders of the Ancient World. It was destroyed by a series of earthquakes in the early fifteenth century. Today, the Scottish Rite Temple in Washington, D.C., is based on its design.

In the following tour of the cemetery's sections, the architectural styles of many structures are noted. That information, which is drawn from a variety of sources, is based on the following brief definitions:

BEAUX-ARTS CLASSICAL. The style represents a blend of Classical designs with elaborate ornamentation ("Beaux-Arts" is French for "fine arts"). It takes its name from the École des Beaux-Arts, a French academy of art and design established in the seventeenth century, which championed the style.

CLASSICAL REVIVAL. A later, more refined stage of the Beaux-Arts style, its designs incorporate elements from Greek and Roman traditions: symmetrical designs and columns topped by Ionic, Doric, or Corinthian order capitals supporting a pediment. Urns are often included as a focal point.

EGYPTIAN REVIVAL. Resplendent with pre-Christian symbolism, the style often features battered (tapered) walls or pylons, flat roofs, hieroglyphics, winged sun disks, and other characteristic symbols. Obelisks also have their origin in Egyptian architecture, symbolizing a ray of sunlight cast on the tomb of a priest or leader. In the Christian tradition, obelisks represent a shaft pointing toward heaven.

GOTHIC REVIVAL. One of the most common styles of architecture found in cemeteries, it often includes asymmetrical designs, buttresses, spires, pointed arches, and stained-glass windows that replicate the characteristics of church buildings. Secular buildings often feature towers, battlements, porches, carriageways, and arched windows.

Bench in front of
the Sage mausoleum
(Classical Revival
style), Bell Tower
Ridge

Obelisk (Egyptian
Revival style)
marking the Hillyer
family lot, Knit Mill

Marsh mausoleum (Gothic Revival style),
Bell Tower Ridge

ROMANESQUE REVIVAL. A design noted for its soaring pyramidal roofs, use of gargoyles or grotesques, buttresses, corbels, round-headed windows, splayed columns, and intricate ornamentation.

RICHARDSONIAN ROMANESQUE. A variation of the Romanesque Revival style, it gained popularity in the late nineteenth century and features stone with a rough, or "rusticated," texture.

ECLECTIC, VERNACULAR, AND EXOTIC REVIVAL. Often seen as reactions to more classical designs, these styles frequently feature a blend of many styles in an individualized expression of the builder's wishes. Stonework may be rough or smooth, while ornamentation may be either absent or unusual.

Bell Tower (Gothic Revival) and Maddox mausoleum (Romanesque Revival), Bell Tower Ridge

Grant mausoleum (Eclectic style), Bell Tower Ridge

Funerary Symbolism

Oakland Cemetery contains excellent examples of the rich array of funerary symbols found carved into gravestones in Victorian-era cemeteries throughout the world. The myriad symbols at Oakland, from crosses and anchors to urns and shrouds, reflect a dramatic period of change in the Christian interpretation of death, ranging from the Puritans' fear of its inevitability to the Victorians' sense of acceptance. The widespread use of the word "cemetery" during this time suggested that death was a transition—a time of "blessed sleep" before the departed would again be reunited in the afterlife.

The naturalistic designs of rural garden cemeteries offered space for elaborate markers, tombs, mausoleums, and monuments. People of the period were greatly influenced by the pioneering archeological work of the day; structures unearthed in Mesopotamia, Egypt, Greece, and the lands of the former Roman Empire captured the popular imagination. In addition, Victorians became enamored with the use of symbolism as a means of expressing their religious beliefs, aspirations, hopes for redemption, or final wishes through iconography. (Iconography can be thought of as an organized system of symbols.)

A cross and anchor adorning the
William Nicholls monument, Knit Mill

A symbol is something that represents or stands for something else. Much funerary symbolism is familiar—a cross or a Star of David, for example—but there are also symbols carved on markers or monuments that convey information about the age, occupation, and social status, among other things, of the person buried there. While even the humblest of the dead might have a cherished symbol such as a cross and crown carved on their gravestone, affluent families saw their elaborate monuments or mausoleums as expressions of their spiritual beliefs as well as a reminder of their worldly wealth.

Oakland Cemetery was established only two decades after the development of America's early rural garden cemeteries, so it represents an excellent example of the evolution of this concept from its formative years through its pinnacle at the end of the nineteenth century. In addition, many of the sacred symbols found here were part of a widely shared iconography. As a result, a visitor from anywhere in the Western world who was knowledgeable about funerary symbolism could visit the cemetery and, to some degree, decipher the stories of its inhabitants. It is also important, as Richard Waterhouse, a former Oakland volunteer, noted in

An angel on the grave of Carmel Quinn,
Bell Tower Ridge

Mourning shroud draping the grave of Mabel Haynes,
Original Six Acres

his book *Sacred Symbols of Oakland* that "in our enthusiasm for the symbols and their meanings and the artistry of the monuments, we remember, as well, those whose gravesites we study."[3] A stroll around Oakland's grounds is an enjoyable pastime, and the ability to "read the stones" offers a greater understanding of the sites and scenes, revealing the humanity of those interred here.

There are several excellent guides to funerary symbolism available to enhance the viewer's understanding. One that is especially useful is *Stories in Stone: A Field Guide to Cemetery Symbolism and Iconography*, by Douglas Keister. A list of important symbols and their meanings is found in appendix A.

Epitaphs

Benjamin Franklin said, "Show me your cemeteries and I will tell you what kind of people you have."[4] The inscriptions that grace many of the monuments and markers in Oakland Cemetery make clear Franklin's observation. Whether brief or rambling, poignant or amusing, an epitaph offers insights into the life of the deceased.

The word "epitaph" comes from the Greek "*epi*" and "*taphos*," meaning "at, over" and "tomb." Thus, an epitaph is an inscription on a tombstone, one intended to memorialize the decedent and serve as "a permanent document of sentiment"—in fact, "the expression of such sentiment is the essence of commemoration."[5]

While epitaphs in one form or another date back to the sarcophagi of ancient Egypt and the tombs of Greece and Rome, the French thanatologist Philippe Ariès noted that "the practice of marking the exact site of a grave by means of an inscription did not become widespread until the end of the eighteenth century."[6] Founded in 1850 during a burgeoning era of romanticism and ritualism, Oakland Cemetery is a model of this cultural movement dedicated to providing a lasting memorial for a loved one.

Poignant epitaph on the grave of Susan Ellis, Knit Mill

Epitaphs come from different sources and serve many purposes. In "Epitaphs and Personality Revelation," Joseph Edgette identified four general categories within which most epitaphs fall:[7]

SCRIPTURE. These are passages from the Bible or other sacred texts that reflect the influence of religious beliefs upon the deceased or those left behind.

POETIC VERSE. These words may reveal contemporary views and attitudes about the nature of death, often in terms of the loss felt by survivors. The words often express acceptance of the loss with a hope for future reunion. Inscriptions may be excerpts from popular poems of the day or original verse crafted by the deceased, a loved one, or even a commissioned monument poet.

VERBAL UTTERANCES. These epitaphs are meant to convey grief over the loss while often expressing a level of acceptance and a hope of reunion.

> *Have pity upon me, have pity upon me, O ye my friends; for the hand of God hath touched me.*
> —Job 19:21
> DANIEL FLECK, KNIT MILL, BLOCK 1

LAND OF MY ADOPTION WHERE
THE LOVED SLEEP FOLDED IN THE
EMBRACE OF YOUR FLOWERS, WOULD THAT IT
WERE MY DESTINY TO INCREASE THE FLOOD
TIDE OF YOUR GLORY AS IT HAS BEEN MINE TO
SHARE YOUR FORTUNES: FOR WHEN MY YEARS
TREMBLE TO THEIR CLOSE, I WOULD SLEEP
BENEATH YOUR SOIL WHERE THE
DRIP OF APRIL TEARS MAY FALL
UPON MY GRAVE: AND THE SUNSHINE
OF YOUR SKIES WARM SOUTHERN FLOWERS
TO BLOOM UPON MY BREAST.

ORIGINAL EXPRESSIONS. Often chosen by the deceased before death or by loved ones, these brief statements may reveal facets of the deceased person's personality and character. They may be both poignant and humorous, sure to catch the eye of passersby.

In addition, we include a fifth category, one not noted by Edgette.

GRAPHIC DESCRIPTIONS. These are often short narratives that describe the circumstances of the individual's death.

By taking time to read the many powerful, poignant, and sometimes humorous epitaphs found on the cemetery's markers and monuments, you will be, for a brief moment, connected to the lives, loves, and cherished memories of those interred within its hallowed grounds.

Even though nearly seventy thousand people are buried in Oakland Cemetery, there are only about thirty thousand monuments. For some of the deceased, such as those in Potters' Field, a marker was never placed. Other markers have been worn down by the ravages of time or, in some instances, lost to vandalism. Through the ongoing preservation efforts of the Historic Oakland Foundation, the remaining gravestones and monuments, many bearing thoughtfully chosen epitaphs, will remain a lasting legacy, memorializing those buried within Oakland's walls.

Three

Exploring Oakland Cemetery

A Tour by Sections

Dead men may tell no tales,
but their tombstones do.
DOUGLAS KEISTER,
Stories in Stone

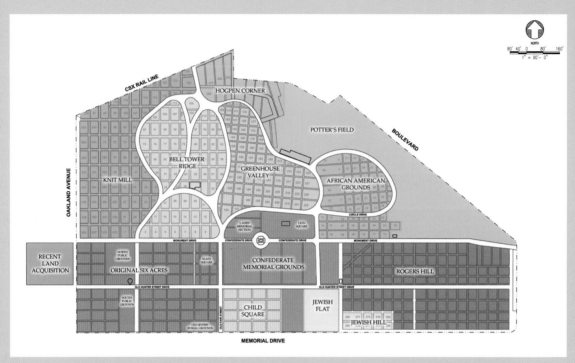

Oakland character sections map

FROM TREE-SHADED LOTS lined with tombstones, monuments, and mausoleums nestled beneath Atlanta's evolving skyline to fields of simple markers lined row on row with military precision, and open meadows that invite quiet contemplation, Oakland Cemetery is a place of storied history and multiple personalities.

Oakland's significance as a nineteenth-century municipal graveyard that was transformed into a model rural garden cemetery is evident throughout its forty-eight landscaped acres. Through the following section tours, we invite the visitor to enjoy the landscaped grounds, interpret and admire the cemetery's funerary art and architecture, with their remarkable examples of sacred symbolism, and pause to read the many poignant and powerful epitaphs that reflect individual sentiments or heartfelt beliefs about death and the afterlife.

Several years ago, in an effort to better delineate Oakland's varied landscapes and historic spaces, the Historic Oakland Foundation developed a nomenclature to describe the different geographic sections of the cemetery. Some of the names, such as Original Six Acres, Confederate Memorial Grounds, Jewish Hill, African American Grounds, Greenhouse Valley, and Potters' Field, express direct connections to the history of the area or its inhabitants. Others, such as Knit Mill, Child Square, Rogers Hill, and Hogpen Corner, leave the visitor to conjecture about their origins.

(Note: Cemetery burial records are based on the division of the cemetery into numerical sections, and these do not correspond to the descriptive titles used by the foundation. For those interested in searching the burial records, a map showing the numerical sections of Oakland is in appendix B.)

> *Say not "Good night," but in some fairer clime,*
> *Bid us "Good morning."*
> —Adapted from Anna Letitia Barbauld, "Life"
> IDA LEE BENNETT BASS, KNIT MILL, BLOCK 2

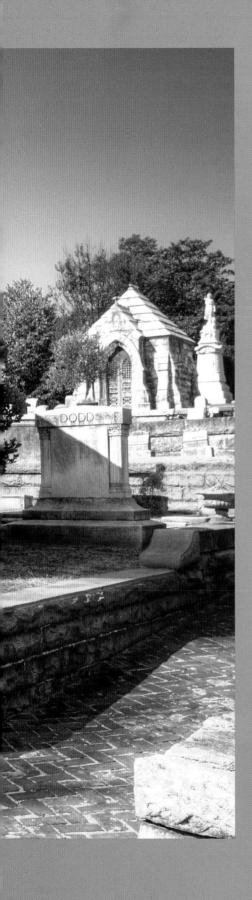

Original
Six Acres

IN 1849, the Atlanta City Council

recognized that a small burial ground on

Peachtree Road north of town was both

inadequate for its purpose and an obstacle

to the city's growth, so a committee was

appointed to search for suitable ground

for a new cemetery. In June 1850, after

examining several sites, the council

authorized the purchase of six acres of

rolling farmland land east of the city

limits from Alfred W. Wooding for

seventy-five dollars an acre. Within the

current cemetery, these original six acres are located north and south of the Main Gate on Martin Luther King Jr. Drive.

Initially, the property was subdivided into lots that were sold for ten dollars each. Two public grounds, one on the north and another on the south, were set aside for travelers' and paupers' burials. A sec-tion at the far eastern end of the cemetery was intended for the segregated interment of slaves and free blacks. By 1857, additional land was needed for the growing city, and four sloping acres east of the burial ground were acquired from James Seavy. In 1860, the city sold six lots to David Mayer, the president of the Hebrew Benevolent Association, to provide a separate burial space for Jewish interments, one that would be consecrated in accordance with Jewish rites and traditions.

Many of Atlanta's pioneer settlers are interred in this section. Included among them are Martha Lumpkin Compton, the daughter of Governor Wilson Lumpkin (the city was named Marthasville in her honor in 1842, and renamed Atlanta in 1845); and Sarah Todd Ivy, the widow of the city's first settler, Hardy Ivy.

Notable Inhabitants
and Structures

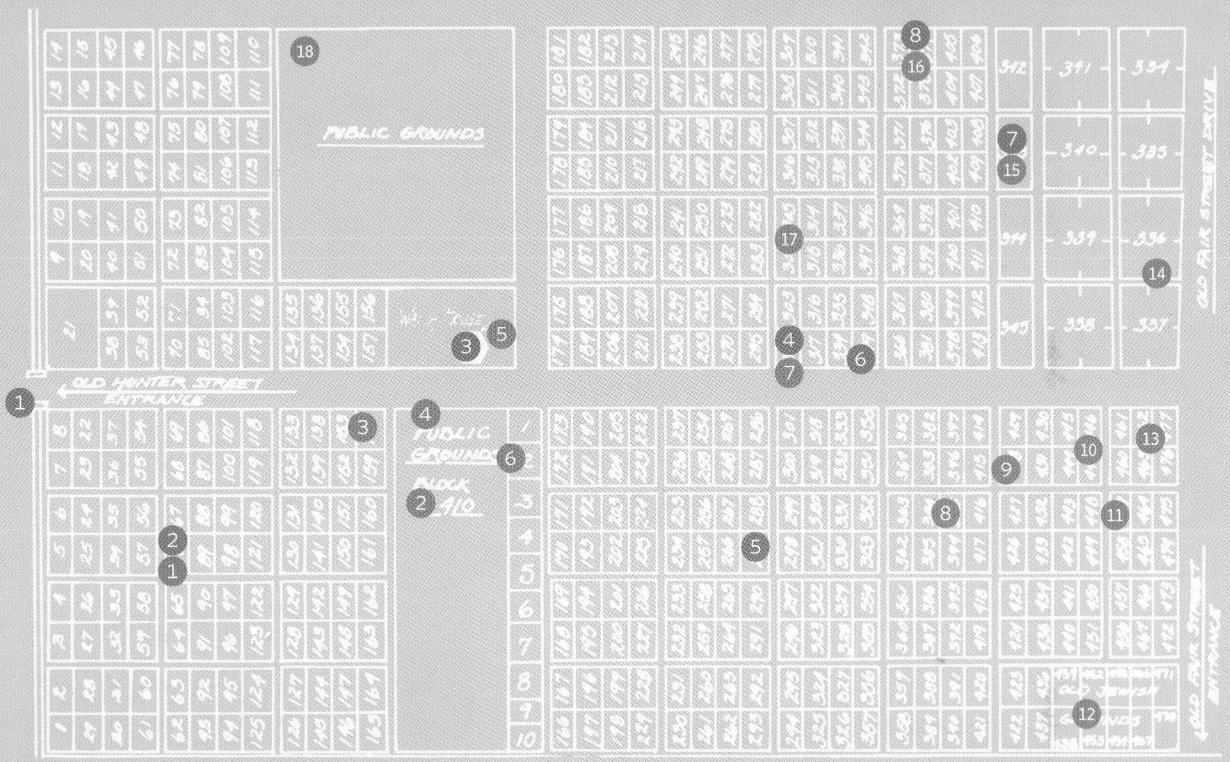

NOTABLE INHABITANTS

NOTABLE STRUCTURES

① Oakland Entrance Portal (1894)

At the Martin Luther King Jr. Drive entrance to the cemetery. The brick portal and enclosing wall were erected before the Cotton States and International Exposition of 1895.

② Dr. James Nissen (d. 1850)

WEST OF THE SOUTH PUBLIC GROUNDS

A physician who was traveling through Atlanta when he became ill and died, Nissen was treated by the pioneer Atlanta doctor Noel P. P. D'Alvigny. Nissen is believed to have been the first direct interment in the new cemetery.

③ Sarah Todd Ivy (d. 1865)

BLOCK 158

Sarah Todd Ivy was the widow of Hardy Ivy, the first settler in what would become Atlanta. His final resting place is unknown (see the sidebar in the Hogpen Corner and Greenhouse Valley section tour).

① ② Jasper Newton Smith Mausoleum

BLOCK 66, ECLECTIC STYLE

It has been said that Smith (d. 1913), an Atlanta building contractor, brickworks owner, and one-time city councilman, refused to wear neckties; thus, the unusual statue of him seated above the door of his crypt depicts him in a suit—but no tie. Because Smith's mausoleum lies so close to the cemetery's main entrance, he has been dubbed the "Mayor of Oakland."

④ Martha Lumpkin Compton (d. 1917)

SOUTH PUBLIC GROUNDS ACROSS FROM THE WATCH HOUSE

Compton was the daughter of Governor Wilson Lumpkin and the namesake of Marthasville.

③ Watch House (1901)

ENTRANCE DRIVE, GOTHIC REVIVAL STYLE

Designed to complement the style of the entrance gate and walls, this structure was originally painted white, like the Bell Tower.

"LEST WE FORGET"

"GREATER LOVE HATH
NO MAN THAN THIS,
THAT A MAN
LAY DOWN HIS LIFE
FOR HIS FRIENDS"

⑤ *Franklin M. Garrett (d. 2000)*

NORTH PUBLIC GROUNDS BESIDE THE WATCH HOUSE

Garrett was a Coca-Cola executive, a longtime president of the Atlanta Historical Society, and the author of *Atlanta and its Environs*. For many years, he was considered "Atlanta's Official Historian" (see the sidebar in chapter 1). Garrett spent more than fifty years compiling a necrology of Atlanta's cemeteries. The information he gathered is available online from the Kenan Research Center at the Atlanta History Center.

There is a day of sunny rest
For every dark and troubled night:
And grief may hide an evening guest,
But joy shall come with early light.

—William Cullen Bryant,
"Blessed Are They That Mourn"

MRS. A. N. WILSON, BLOCK 460

⑥ *Carrie Berry Crumley (d. 1921)*

BLOCK 2

The diary kept by ten-year-old Crumley in 1864 provides a powerful firsthand account of a Southern family during the Civil War (see the sidebar in chapter 1).

⑦ ④ *Judge John Collier Mausoleum*

BLOCK 302, ECLECTIC

Judge Collier (d. 1892) was the son of Meredith Collier and the brother of George Washington Collier, two of Atlanta's earliest settlers. He authored Atlanta's first city charter (1847) and Fulton County's first charter (1853).

⑤ *Christian Kontz Monument (1909)*

BLOCK 289, EGYPTIAN REVIVAL

This unusual monument, commissioned by Christian Kontz (d. 1881) and erected by his family, incorporates both pagan and Christian symbolism.

⑥ Thomas Neal Family Monument (ca. 1890s)

BLOCK 349, NEOCLASSICAL

Thomas Neal, the surviving son of John Neal (buried nearby), erected this poignant memorial to his wife and daughter. Neal served in the Confederate army and was captured at the Battle of Vicksburg, 1863.

> *I would sleep beneath your soil where the drip of April tears may fall upon my grave; and the sunshine of your skies warm Southern flowers to bloom upon my breast.*
>
> JUDGE OSBORNE LOCHRANE, BLOCK 336

⑧ James Calhoun (d. 1875)

BLOCK 395

A member of the Georgia General Assembly in 1837 and State Senate in 1851, Calhoun was elected mayor of Atlanta in 1862 and served four one-year terms. He surrendered the city to Sherman's army on September 2, 1864. He was a cousin of South Carolina senator John C. Calhoun.

James Calhoun, ca. 1860s

9 Dye Family Lot
BLOCK 428

Sarah Dye (d. 1888) braved the shelling of Atlanta to travel to the cemetery to bury her two-year-old son, John, on July 20, 1864.

10 John Neal Family Lot
BLOCKS 446–447

The lot contains the remains of John Neal (d. 1886) and Mary Neal (d. 1896), whose house on Hunter Street served as General Sherman's headquarters during the Union occupation in 1864. (According to local lore, he refused to live in the house again.) Interred next to them are the bodies of two sons, James H. Neal (d. 1865) and Andrew Jackson Neal (d. 1864), both killed during the Civil War. Note the military symbols on each of their graves.

Erected by myself.
VIRGINIA HAMPTON FOSTER, WHO OUTLIVED HER FAMILY, BLOCK 174

11 Agnes Wooding (d. 1850)
BLOCK 459

The wife of A. W. Wooding, she was interred on this site before Wooding sold the land to the city for the cemetery, making her Oakland's first interment. Her husband, who died in 1878, is buried beside her.

12 Old Jewish Burial Ground (1860)
MULTIPLE BLOCKS, 438–471

Property for this burial space was acquired from the city by David Mayer, the president of the Hebrew Benevolent Association. The site is among the oldest Jewish burial grounds in Georgia (the oldest is in Savannah), and Jews from across the state and region were interred here.

Richard Peters Family Lot
BLOCKS 462–477

A Pennsylvania native, Peters (d. 1889) was a pioneer Atlanta settler, and is often credited with promoting the name "Atlanta" for the city. Peters was a successful railroad executive and developer. In 1871, he built Atlanta's first street railway, and went on to promote the development of Midtown Atlanta. Peters was a founding benefactor of the Georgia School of Technology (Georgia Tech).

Catherine Holmes (d. 1896)
BLOCK 336

Holmes was a former slave and later a domestic servant employed by the Boylston family. The family received permission to have her interred in the family's lot.

Abner Calhoun Mausoleum
BLOCK 343, CLASSICAL REVIVAL

Dr. Calhoun (d. 1883), the first scientifically trained ear, nose, and throat specialist in Georgia, established that department of studies at the Atlanta Medical College (a predecessor of the Emory University School of Medicine).

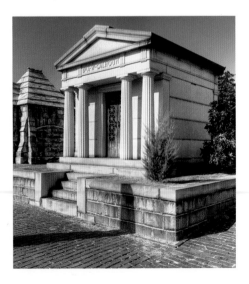

Alfred Austell Mausoleum
BLOCK 374, GOTHIC REVIVAL

A railroad builder and banker, Austell (d. 1881) came to Atlanta in 1858. He served as president of the postwar Atlanta National Bank, now part of Wells Fargo. The city of Austell is named for him. Also interred in the family mausoleum are Albert Thornton (d. 1907), Austell's son-in-law and the president of Elberton Oil Mills, as well as Alfred D. Kennedy (d. 1983), a banker and developer. The mausoleum cost $16,000 to construct and was, at the time, the most expensive structure in Oakland Cemetery.

Alfred Austell, ca. 1870s.

W AUSTIN
LEYDEN
MAJOR
9 GA
LIGHT ARTY
CSA
1826
1900

Judge Ruben Cone (d. 1851)

BLOCKS 304–305

Born in 1788, Cone came to Decatur in 1823, where he served as an original town commissioner and judge. He later acquired several hundred acres of land in what would become downtown Atlanta. He laid out Marietta Street and built his home there. (It would later become a hotel.) The zero milepost, set by the engineer Stephen H. Long in 1837, was located on Judge Cone's property (DeKalb County Land Lot no. 78).

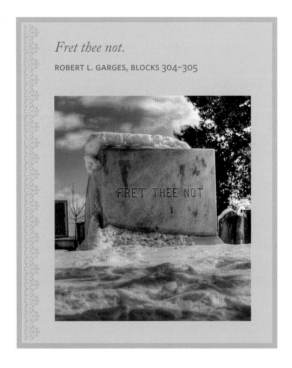

Fret thee not.

ROBERT L. GARGES, BLOCKS 304–305

The Deceased was an Engineer and was accidentally killed on the Atlanta and LaGrange Railroad while in the discharge of his duty. He was noted for his piety and morality and was beloved by all who knew him.

ISAAC SMITH, BLOCK 55

Maynard H. Jackson Jr. (d. 2003)

NORTH PUBLIC GROUNDS

Jackson was elected mayor of Atlanta in 1973, becoming the first African American to govern a major southern city. He served three terms, 1974–82 and 1990–94, and was instrumental in bringing the 1996 Olympic Games to Atlanta. His father, Maynard Jackson Sr., served as the minister of Friendship Baptist Church (Atlanta's oldest black congregation). Mayor Jackson was the grandson of John Wesley Dobbs, a pioneering civil rights advocate. Following the unexpected death of Jackson in 2003, the City of Atlanta, with support from the Historic Oakland Foundation, extended an invitation to the Jackson family for his interment in a space available in Oakland's North Public Grounds. Recognizing his role in the civil rights movement as well as in Atlanta's history, the foundation's staff and board members believed that this act would symbolize the final breaking of the color line within Oakland's Original Six Acres.

Maynard Jackson, ca. 1990s

End of the Trail

ONE OF OAKLAND CEMETERY'S more unusual and powerful monuments is the memorial for Benjamin F. Perry Jr., who died in 1933 at the age of fifty (block 306). The bas-relief sculpture on Perry's gravestone is based on artist James Earl Fraser's work *End of the Trail*, which was produced for San Francisco's Panama-Pacific International Exposition in 1915.

End of the Trail grave marker of Ben F. Perry

A South Dakota native, Fraser grew up in the late nineteenth century and witnessed with sadness what some described as the "doomed fate" of the once-proud Plains Indians. Fraser went on to study at the Art Institute of Chicago and later in Paris. There, his first version of this work, completed in 1898, won the John Wanamaker Prize from the American Artists Association.

Fraser continued to refine the work, and the monumental version, cast in plaster, graced the central grounds of the San Francisco exposition, where it was viewed by thousands of fairgoers. In 1919, the sculpture was acquired by the residents of Tulare County, California, and placed in a local park. Nearly fifty years later, the National Cowboy and Western Heritage Museum, in Oklahoma City, had a bronze cast made from the original and placed on display in its exhibition hall.

In addition to this sculpture, Fraser may be best known as the designer of the Buffalo Head nickel, which was produced by the United States Mint from 1913 to 1938. These coins, considered of exceptional design quality, are highly prized by collectors.

The placement of this evocative sculpture, with its epitaph "End of Trail," on Perry's memorial seems especially poignant when the viewer learns that he died by his own hand.

Other Significant Inhabitants and Structures

Austin Leyden (d. 1900). Born in Pennsylvania, Leyden came to Atlanta as a twenty-two-year-old in 1848 and opened the city's first foundry. His Atlanta Machine Works would make him one of the city's wealthiest residents. The Leyden home on Peachtree was among Atlanta's most elegant structures and served as headquarters for General George Thomas during the 1864 Union occupation. During the war, Major Leyden commanded a Confederate artillery battery under General James Longstreet. (Block 313)

Benjamin F. Bomar (d. 1868). A pioneer Atlanta physician, clerk of the superior court, and the second mayor of Atlanta, 1849. (Blocks 84–85)

Benjamin Dewberry (d. 1908). A locomotive engineer killed in a railroad accident that inspired the popular song "Ben Dewberry's Last Ride." (Block 474)

Daniel Lynch (d. 1871). A volunteer fireman who became Atlanta's first firefighter to die in the line of duty. (Block 448)

Dodd Mausoleum (Classical Revival). Green P. Dodd (d. 1905) and Philip G. Dodd (d. 1911) operated a general store in Atlanta from the 1850s. (Block 335)

Floyd McRae (d. 1921). Dr. McRae was a noted surgeon, a son-in-law of Judge John Collier, and a founder of Piedmont Hospital. (Block 302)

Harwick-Luckie-Hemmer Mausoleum (Classical Revival). This structure, erected in 1978, contains the remains of the poet Eugene Thaddeus Luckie (d. 1932), often called the "Georgia (Robert) Burns." (Block 212)

James E. Williams (d. 1900). The first mayor elected after the Civil War, serving 1866–69. On July 22, 1864, the Confederate general John B. Hood watched the Battle of Atlanta from the Williams home (note the state historical marker north of the Bell Tower). (Block 415)

John F. Mims (d. 1856). A railroad banker and the mayor of Atlanta in 1856. (Block 217)

Joseph Winship (d. 1878). A pioneer Atlanta settler and the owner of Winship Machine Works and Continental Gin Company. His sons Robert (d. 1899) and George (d. 1916) are buried in the Bell Tower Ridge section. (Block 271)

Marcus Aurelius Bell (d. 1885). A son of the pioneer Atlanta settler James Bell, he owned the "Calico House," which was used as a Civil War hospital and later as Wesley Memorial Hospital (predecessor of Emory University Hospital). (Block 272)

Michael Kenny (d. 1870). One of the many Irish immigrants who settled in early Atlanta, Kenny operated a saloon in what became known as "Kenny's Alley" (now part of Underground Atlanta). (Block 27)

Nellie Peters Black (d. 1919). An educator and social activist, Black was the daughter of the pioneer settler Richard Peters. She was named a Georgia Woman of Achievement in 1996. (Block 477)

Osborne Lochrane (d. 1887). A pioneer Atlantan, lawyer, and associate justice of the State Supreme Court. (Block 336)

Ragan Mausoleum (Romanesque Revival). Erected for the wholesale dry-goods merchant Willis E. Ragan (d. 1916). (Block 343)

Stephens Mitchell (d. 1983). A prominent Atlanta attorney and the elder brother of the author Margaret Mitchell. (Block 390)

Venable Mausoleum (Eclectic). William R. Venable (d. 1873) was a pioneer Atlanta settler and a clerk of the Fulton County Superior Court. His sons William H. and Samuel H. Venable were longtime owners of Stone Mountain and operated a granite quarry on the mountain's eastern slope. Samuel Venable was associated with the second founding of the Ku Klux Klan in November 1915. He gave the KKK permission to hold its rallies and ritual cross burnings on Stone Mountain. He also granted permission to the United Daughters of the Confederacy for the carving on the north face of the mountain. Samuel is in the mausoleum with his father. (Mausoleum Block 243)

William Ezzard (d. 1887). A pioneer settler and a mayor of Atlanta, 1856–57 and 1870. He coined the term "Gate City Guard" in 1857. (Block 208)

Beloved he lived, and, ending life's brief span,
Beloved he died, at peace with God and Man
—Arthur Peterson, "The Divan"
EUGENE HINTON, BLOCK 159

Knit Mill

THIS SECTION in the northwestern
corner of Oakland Cemetery may take its
name from the nineteenth-century Atlanta
Hosiery Mill that was located just west
of the cemetery grounds. The two-story
brick building that once housed the mill,
now adapted for use as loft apartments,
is visible beyond the cemetery's wall. This
area, adjacent to the railroad line, was
the site of a number of mills, factories,
and other industrial businesses. During a
century of industrial operations beginning

in the 1870s, the mills were bustling, with hundreds of employees and their families occupying a collection of surrounding frame houses, the last of which was destroyed by fire in 2007.

Much of the property for this section of the cemetery was assembled through purchases in 1866–67 from Alfred W. Wooding, Salina Boling, and Lewis Schofield, a former owner of the nearby Atlanta Rolling Mill (destroyed in 1864). Knit Mill is noted as the final resting place for such notable Atlantans as the author Margaret Mitchell Marsh, the developer Joel Hurt, Georgia governors Joseph Emerson Brown and his son Joseph Mackey Brown, and Benjamin Franklin White, the composer of the *Sacred Harp* songbook (1844).

Notable Inhabitants
and Structures

NOTABLE INHABITANTS

NOTABLE STRUCTURES

① Hibernian Benevolent Society Ground

BLOCK 233

This plot of ground in the cemetery was deeded by the City of Atlanta in 1873 to commemorate the Civil War service of the Hibernian Rifles and the memory of Father Thomas O'Reilly, the pastor of the Shrine of the Immaculate Conception, who ministered to the wounded of both armies in Atlanta's crowded hospitals.

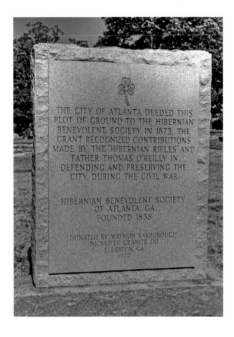

First Bag Man.

PIAMUS JONES, BLOCK 240. HE IS BELIEVED TO HAVE BEEN A FOUNDING MEMBER OF ATLANTA'S FIRST BASEBALL TEAM, AND HIS EPITAPH MAY INDICATE THE POSITION HE PLAYED.

① Margaret Mitchell Marsh (d. 1949)

BLOCK 22

Margaret "Peggy" Mitchell was born in Atlanta in 1900. As a child, she listened to stories about the Civil War from her grandfather, the Confederate veteran Russell Mitchell, and visited her maternal grandfather Philip Fitzgerald's antebellum farm in Clayton County. These stories provided the foundation for her Pulitzer Prize–winning novel, *Gone With the Wind*, published in 1936. The film version, starring Clark Gable and Vivien Leigh, had its world premiere in Atlanta in December 1939 and remains one of the most popular films ever made. Mitchell died in Atlanta's Grady Hospital in 1949 after being struck by an automobile while crossing Peachtree Street not far from her apartment on Crescent Avenue (now the Margaret Mitchell House museum) where she penned her novel. Her grave is among the cemetery's most visited sites, and for many years, her publisher furnished tulip bulbs from Holland to be planted at her grave site. She was named a Georgia Woman of Achievement in 1994 and was inducted into the Georgia Writers Hall of Fame in 2000.

Margaret Mitchell, ca. 1936

2 Anthony Murphy (d. 1909)
BLOCK 42

Murphy, a foreman for the Western and Atlantic Railroad during the Civil War, was aboard the locomotive "General" the day it was stolen by Union raiders in April 1862. He joined the pursuit of the stolen engine in the "Texas," participating in what is now called the "Great Locomotive Chase." His fellow pursuers—William Fuller, the conductor, and Jeff Cain, an engineer—are also buried at Oakland.

3 Clayton, Nicolson, and Hoge Families Lot
BLOCK 47

As a teenager during the Civil War, Sarah (Sallie) Clayton (d. 1922) penned the diary that inspired the memoir *Requiem for a Lost City*, a powerful eyewitness account of the Battle of Atlanta. Her sister Augusta (Gussie) died in 1864 from typhoid contracted while working in the war hospitals. Sallie's sister Julia (d. 1909) married Edward Hoge (d. 1885), the founder of the *Atlanta Journal* newspaper. Sallie's daughter Carolyn (d. 1949) married Dr. William Perrin Nicolson (d. 1928), a prominent Atlanta physician.

4 Brigadier General Lucius Gartrell (d. 1891)
BLOCK 47

Gartrell, an attorney, served in the state legislature and later as a member of Congress. He resigned from Congress in 1861 to form the Seventh Georgia Infantry Regiment in the Confederate army. He also served in the Confederate Congress (1862–64) before returning to military service. Gartrell's home, once located just north of the Georgia Railroad, served briefly as Confederate general John B. Hood's temporary headquarters during the Battle of Atlanta, July 1864.

5 Joel Hurt (d. 1926)
BLOCK 237

A prominent Atlanta real estate developer, Hurt developed the city's first planned suburb, Inman Park (named for his friend and business associate Samuel Inman, who is buried at Oakland), as well as the Atlanta and Edgewood Street Railway, the city's first electric streetcar line. (Horse- and mule-drawn lines began service in 1871.)

Joel Hurt, ca. 1920s

6 Julia Carlisle Withers (d. 1919)
BLOCK 72

Born in 1842, she is often called "Atlanta's first baby," although she was born in Marietta.

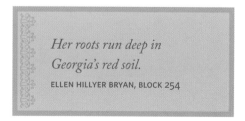

Her roots run deep in Georgia's red soil.
ELLEN HILLYER BRYAN, BLOCK 254

7 **2** *William Fuller (d. 1905)*

BLOCK 72, EGYPTIAN REVIVAL

Fuller was the conductor on the "General" when the locomotive was stolen by James J. Andrews and a group of raiders in April 1862. He organized the pursuit aboard the engine "Texas," capturing the Union soldiers outside Ringgold, Georgia. Railroad workers were exempt from Confederate military service, but Fuller was awarded an honorary captaincy for his role in what has come to be called the Great Locomotive Chase.

8 **3** *Joseph E. Brown Family Lot*

BLOCK 99

Marked by a magnificent Classical Revival monument topped by a statue of the archangel Gabriel, this lot is the final resting place for two Georgia governors. Joseph E. Brown (d. 1894) served four terms and was the Civil War governor of Georgia; his son, Joseph M. Brown (d. 1932), served two terms as governor, 1909–11 and 1912–13. A statue of Governor Joseph E. Brown, accompanied by his wife, Elizabeth, can be found on the grounds of the Georgia State Capitol.

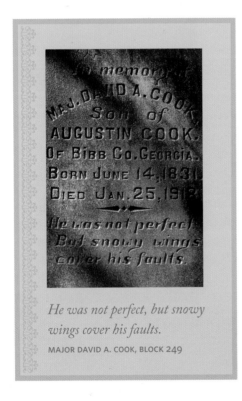

He was not perfect, but snowy wings cover his faults.

MAJOR DAVID A. COOK, BLOCK 249

Her spotless soul unfettered flies— to greet our baby in the skies.

MAY PINCKNEY, BLOCK 230

Joseph E. Brown, ca. 1890s

Major Benjamin Franklin White and The Sacred Harp

BORN IN Union County, South Carolina, in 1800, Benjamin Franklin White grew up in the traditions of gospel singing and camp meetings. While his formal education was limited to less than a year of school, he had an aptitude for music and mastered all the music books he could find. He also learned to play several instruments and served as a fife player in the South Carolina militia during the War of 1812.

He married Thurza Golightly in 1825, and together they raised nine children. In 1835, he collaborated with his brother-in-law William Walker in compiling a collection of hymns that were published as *The Southern Harmony and Musical Companion*. The book was very popular, but White was disappointed when Walker claimed all the credit for its production.

In May 1842, White and his family traveled by wagon to their new home in Harris County, Georgia, where he purchased a ninety-five-acre farm near Whitesville. During his years in Harris County, White taught music at the Hamilton Female Institute, worked as clerk of the inferior court, was elected a major in the Georgia militia, and served as editor of the *Organ*, a weekly newspaper "devoted to art, science, education, morality, and the advancement of sacred music."

B. F. White's descendants at Oakland, ca. 1911

Music was his passion, and shortly after arriving in Georgia, he began compiling hymns for a new tune book, this time using "shape notes" that could be easily followed for congregational singing. White enlisted the aid of a gifted young student, Elisha King, in this work, and together they wrote *The Sacred Harp*. Sadly, King died in August 1844, two months before the songbook's publication. The book was an immediate success. The following year, White organized the Southern Musical Convention; he published expanded editions of *The Sacred Harp* in 1850, 1859, and 1869.

Following the Civil War, Benjamin and Thurza White moved to DeKalb County, Georgia, to be close to their children and grandchildren. Thurza died in 1878, and Benjamin followed in 1879. Both were interred at Oakland Cemetery. Shortly before his death, he sang the hymn "Sounding Joy," which he had written for the 1859 edition of *The Sacred Harp*. One stanza seems fitting as the visitor views his final resting place:

> But when the gospel comes,
> It spreads diviner light,
> It calls all sinners from their tombs,
> And gives the blind their sight.

Benjamin Franklin White (d. 1879)

BLOCK 125

Born in South Carolina in 1800, White and his wife, Thurza, moved to Harris County, Georgia, in 1842. He was an educator, journalist, court clerk, and composer. In 1844, he and Elisha King wrote *The Sacred Harp*, a book of hymns utilizing shape notes. After King's death in 1844, White saw the songbook through four more editions and was recognized as a master in the art of shape-note singing.

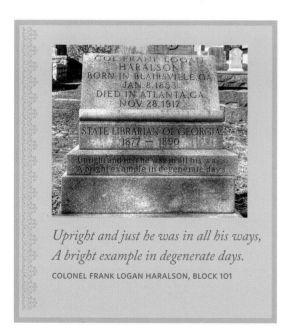

Upright and just he was in all his ways,
A bright example in degenerate days.

COLONEL FRANK LOGAN HARALSON, BLOCK 101

Waid Hill Family Mauseoleum

BLOCK 124

Among the oldest mausoleums at Oakland, this simple brick structure was thought to have been erected sometime in the 1870s. Little was known about the occupants of the "mystery vault" until the 1930s, when a descendant of the original owner, Waid Hill (d. 1876), provided a brief family history. The site is also marked by family tragedy. According to the family, two of Hill's grandsons, the brothers R. P. Hill and O. C. Hill, fell in love with the same young woman. In November 1886, they locked themselves in a room in a drunken rage. One brother killed the other and then turned the gun on himself. Both died from their wounds and now rest together in an unmarked grave outside the walls of the crypt.

Born at Cedartown GA
May 4th 1862
Died at Atlanta
March 20th, 1872
From having his arm
Crushed by an engine of
The GA R.R. in sight
Of where he now rests.

NORRIS BROYLES, BLOCK 2

Bloomfield Family. This poignant monument records the tragic deaths from diphtheria of four daughters in less than two weeks during January 1863. (Block 230)

Junius and George Hillyer. Junius (d. 1886) was a prominent attorney and member of Congress. His son, George (d. 1927), also an attorney and a judge in the Fulton County Superior Court, served as mayor of Atlanta, 1885–86. (Block 254)

Charles W. Hubner (d. 1929). During the Civil War, Hubner was in charge of the telegraph service for the Confederate Army of Tennessee. On July 17, 1864, he delivered the telegram from President Jefferson Davis to General Joseph E. Johnston that relieved the general of command of the army before the Battle of Atlanta. After the war, Hubner became a newspaper editor and writer, penning eleven books of poetry. He was a friend of the noted literary figures Joel Chandler Harris and Sidney Lanier. In 1909, Hubner was awarded the Poe Medal for his writing and in 1928, at the age of ninety-three, was named poet laureate by the Poetry Society of the South. (Block 98)

Henry H. Green Mausoleum (Eclectic). This structure was erected for the Confederate veteran and Atlanta physician Dr. H. H. Green (d. 1896). The bronze doors were stolen during World War II, but were recovered by his granddaughters and painted black. (Block 255)

Mary Glover Thurman (d. 1916). The wife of the pioneer Atlanta dentist Dr. Fendall Thurman, she was dubbed the "Angel of Atlanta" for her gifts of flowers from her garden to patients in Atlanta's hospitals. The beautiful sculpture of an angel on her tomb is believed to be the work of James Novelli, and was based on Daniel Chester French's Kinsley Memorial in New York's Woodlawn Cemetery. The Thurmans' home was located on West Peachtree Street where the Biltmore Hotel is now. (Block 44)

Rose Mausoleum (Eclectic). Rufus Rose, MD (d. 1910), came to Atlanta in 1867 to practice medicine. He also owned the Four Roses Distillery. (Block 94)

Peel Mausoleum (Classical Revival). This structure is the final resting place of William L. Peel (d. 1927), a banking partner of Robert Maddox and Jett Rucker. His wife, Lucy Cook Peel (d. 1923), was a founding member of the Joseph Habersham Chapter of the Daughters of the American Revolution. (Block 23)

Tweet the mockingbird (d. 1874). Although a lamb marks the location, the grave holds the remains of a family's pet bird. (Block 48)

William A. Hemphill (d. 1902). A mayor of Atlanta (1891–92) and owner of the *Atlanta Constitution*. (Block 73)

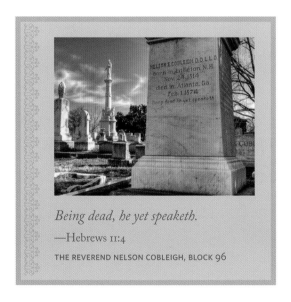

Being dead, he yet speaketh.
—Hebrews 11:4

THE REVEREND NELSON COBLEIGH, BLOCK 96

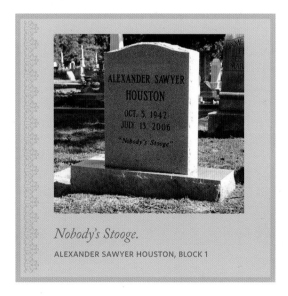

Nobody's Stooge.

ALEXANDER SAWYER HOUSTON, BLOCK 1

Bell Tower Ridge

BELL TOWER RIDGE is the highest ground
within the cemetery and, at 1,070 feet above
sea level, the second-highest naturally
occurring point in the city. The ridge crests
near the Austell mausoleum and descends
toward the northern boundary of the
cemetery, the land sloping away to the east
and west of the ridgeline. This section was
long sought after for its panoramic views
of the surrounding landscape and emerging
city skyline. As a result, it features some of
the cemetery's most elaborate mausoleums

and monuments as well as the 1899 Gothic Revival Bell Tower, which houses a visitor center, the sexton's office, and headquarters for the Historic Oakland Foundation.

At the time of the Civil War, this land lay beyond the northern boundary of the original City Cemetery. On the site was a two-story house owned by James Williams, later mayor of Atlanta (1866–68), which served as an observation post for Confederate general John B. Hood during the Battle of Atlanta on July 22, 1864. Today, a Georgia historical marker notes the site "Where Hood Watched the Battle of Atlanta."

Notable Inhabitants
and Structures

NOTABLE INHABITANTS

NOTABLE STRUCTURES

① Bell Tower

BLOCK 35, GOTHIC REVIVAL

Completed in 1899, the structure originally
contained receiving vaults, offices, a chapel, and
reception rooms. The second floor served as a
residence for the sexton and his family.

① ② James R. Gray (d. 1917)

BLOCK 36

Born in Adairsville, Georgia, in 1859, Gray
moved to Atlanta in 1879 to practice law,
eventually becoming a partner of Judge W.
D. Ellis (buried at Oakland). In 1900, he led
a group in the purchase of the *Atlanta Journal*
newspaper. Five years later, he acquired a
controlling interest in the paper, serving as its
president and editor until his death. In 1881,
he married May Inman, a daughter of Samuel
Inman. The funerary monument above the
graves represents the mourning Niobe of Greek
mythology, whose fourteen children were
murdered by Artemis and Apollo.

Our dearest hopes lie buried here.
ERWIN COLLINS, BLOCK 65

② ③ *Cotting-Burke Vault*

BLOCK 37, ECLECTIC

Interred in the vault are David Cotting (d. 1874), who served as Georgia secretary of state (1868–73), and his brother-in-law Joseph Burke (d. 1927), who was a Confederate veteran and commander of the Gate City Guard in 1911. The body of Alexander H. Stephens, the former congressman, Confederate vice president, and Georgia governor, was placed in this vault following his death in 1883. A year later, his body was removed to the grounds of Liberty Hall, his plantation home near Crawfordville, Georgia (now within Alexander H. Stephens State Park).

④ *Garrett Gas Lamp*

IN LANE WEST OF THE COTTING-BURKE VAULT

One of the original gas lamps erected in Atlanta before the Civil War, it was placed in Oakland to honor the historian Franklin Garrett. The lamppost shows evidence of possible damage from the siege of Atlanta in 1864.

> *When she had passed, it was like the ceasing of exquisite music.*
>
> —Henry Wadsworth Longfellow, "Evangeline"
>
> MARY MARSH CRANKSHAW, BLOCK 61

③ ⑤ *James W. English (d. 1925) Monument*

BLOCK 52, CLASSICAL REVIVAL

Captain English, a Confederate veteran and banker, was elected mayor of Atlanta in 1881. On April 7, 1865, he served as courier for the first correspondence between Ulysses Grant and Robert E. Lee proposing the latter's surrender at Appomattox Courthouse.

⑥ *Mayors Monument*

NORTH OF BLOCK 54

This marble marker lists the names of all mayors of Atlanta, twenty-seven of whom are buried at Oakland.

④ ⑦ *Kiser Mausoleum and Monuments*

BLOCK 90, RICHARDSONIAN ROMANESQUE

At the time of his death, the dry-goods merchant Marion Kiser (d. 1893) was among Atlanta's wealthiest residents. All three of his wives are interred with him in the family crypt (along with his third wife's first husband). The mausoleum, with the rough stone elements characteristic of the Richardsonian Romanesque style, was completed in 1873. The adjacent monument, erected for his brother, John F. Kiser (d. 1882), is topped with a statue of the archangel Gabriel.

⑤ ⑧ *Winship Mausoleum*

BLOCK 108, ECLECTIC

George Winship (d. 1916) was the son of the pioneer Atlantan Joseph Winship (buried at Oakland). The Winship Machine Works provided equipment for the railroads. George Winship's brother, Robert, is buried in the adjacent Hankey family lot. His grandson, Robert Winship Woodruff, led the Coca-Cola Company for more than sixty years.

⑥ ⑨ *Richards Mausoleum*

BLOCK 109, RICHARDSONIAN ROMANESQUE

Robert Richards (d. 1888) was born in England in 1830 and came to America at age fourteen. He arrived in Atlanta in 1850 to work in McPherson's bookstore, the city's first bookseller. After the Civil War, he became involved in banking, textiles, and insurance and rose to become one of the city's wealthiest inhabitants.

Georgia Historical Marker
BLOCK 87

The state historical marker notes the site of the Civil War–era home of James Williams (buried at Oakland), which was used by the Confederate general John B. Hood as an observation post during the Battle of Atlanta. Williams served as Atlanta's mayor from 1866 to 1869.

Judge Logan E. Bleckley (d. 1907)
BLOCK 87

Born in the remote North Georgia Mountains in 1827, Bleckley lacked a formal education yet became one of Georgia's, and the nation's, most respected jurists. He served as chief justice of the Georgia Supreme Court from 1887 to 1894. The unusual grave marker is a stone from his native Rabun County.

Marsh Mausoleum
BLOCK 61, GOTHIC REVIVAL

Edwin W. Marsh (d. 1900) was a prominent dry-goods merchant. His business partner and neighbor William Moore is buried in the same block. The massive bronze urns flanking the mausoleum were cast at the Gorham Foundry in New York. The gazebo behind the mausoleum once stood on the Marsh property and served as a gathering place for both the Marsh and Moore families.

Judge Logan Bleckley, Illustrious Jurist

BORN IN THE RUGGED NORTH GEORGIA MOUNTAINS in 1827, Logan E. Bleckley had virtually no formal education. Yet by age eleven, he was reading legal documents in his father's office in the Rabun County courthouse. Seven years later, the self-educated young man passed the Georgia bar exam and began working as an attorney. In 1847, Bleckley moved to Atlanta to work for the railroad, and in 1853 he was elected solicitor for the Coweta Judicial Circuit, serving for four years.

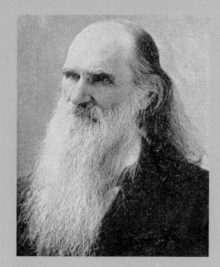

When war broke out, he enlisted in the Confederate army, writing that he was "taking a course in the noble art of homicide," but was discharged for poor health before he saw combat. He returned to Atlanta to practice law, serving as a reporter for the Georgia Supreme Court from 1864 to 1867. During these years, Bleckley was recognized by his colleagues as a gifted attorney with a remarkable capacity to grasp and explain complex legal issues and concepts. Few were surprised when he was appointed associate justice of the state supreme court in 1875. There his skills reached a national audience, and he was acknowledged as one of the nation's preeminent jurists. Interestingly, when he resigned from the court because of ill health in 1880, he remarked that he had never felt "sufficiently learned in the law" to serve on the bench. Nonetheless, in 1887, when Governor John B. Gordon asked him to serve as the court's chief justice, he readily accepted. But his frail health, combined with a crushing workload, forced him to retire in 1894.

He was widely recognized for his flowing white beard, broad sense of humor, love of poetry, and unquenchable thirst for knowledge. (He enrolled in the University of Georgia at age seventy-three to study mathematics.) He died in Clarkesville in 1907 and was buried at Oakland beneath a rough stone from "Screamer Mountain," his beloved Georgia Mountains home. More than a century after his death, he is still considered the most illustrious judge to ever sit on Georgia's highest court. Today, the Atlanta Bar Association bestows the annual Logan E. Bleckley Distinguished Service Award on a local judge who best exemplifies Bleckley's lifelong commitment to the law and public service.

⑨ ⑫ *Maddox Mausoleum*

BLOCK 56, ROMANESQUE REVIVAL

The Confederate veteran, merchant, state representative, and banker Robert Flournoy Maddox (d. 1899) came to Atlanta in 1858. Penniless after the war, he had become one of the city's wealthiest residents by the time of his death. His son, Robert Foster Maddox (d. 1965), served as mayor of Atlanta, 1909–10. In the 1960s, the Maddox family's Buckhead estate was sold to the state of Georgia for construction of the current Governor's Mansion.

Robert F. Maddox, ca. 1920s

⑩ ⑬ *Grant Mausoleum*

BLOCK 57, ECLECTIC

John T. Grant (d. 1887) earned a fortune building railroad lines throughout the South. He was the son-in-law of Hugh T. Inman, a wealthy cotton merchant (interred at Oakland). Grant's grandson, John W. Grant (d. 1938), was a banker and real estate developer. Hugh Inman Grant (d. 1906) was the son of John W. Grant. In his memory, Grant gave funds to Georgia Tech for construction of the football stadium, named Grant Field (now Bobby Dodd Stadium at Historic Grant Field). Also interred here is John Slaton (d. 1955), Georgia's governor in 1911–12 and 1913–15. He was vilified by many Georgians in 1915 for commuting the controversial death sentence of Leo Frank, a Jewish factory manager who had been convicted of the murder of Mary Phagan, a factory employee. Frank was lynched, and Slaton never held public office again; the State of Georgia granted Frank a posthumous pardon in 1986. In addition, the body of the journalist Henry Grady (d. 1889) was briefly placed here while his tomb at Westview Cemetery was under construction. The Grant estate in Buckhead is now part of the Cherokee Town Club.

John Slaton, 1922

Out in the Rain Fountain

BETWEEN BELL TOWER RIDGE AND GREENHOUSE VALLEY

Purchased by the city for $100 in 1913, the fountain is a replica of a fountain displayed at the Centennial Exposition in Philadelphia in 1876. The fountain was relocated and restored in 2008 for $10,000.

She stood four square to all the winds that blew.

—Adapted from Alfred Lord Tennyson, "Ode on the Death of the Duke of Wellington"

JULIA O'KEEFE NELSON, BLOCK 62

Moses Formwalt (d. 1852)

BLOCK 11

Formwalt, an Atlanta pioneer, worked as a copper- and tinsmith. In 1848, he was elected Atlanta's first mayor. After his term as mayor, Formwalt worked as a DeKalb County sheriff's deputy; he was killed in the line of duty in 1852. His body was first interred in the Original Six Acres in an unmarked grave. In 1916, the remains were identified and relocated to this site beneath the monument erected in his honor.

William Markham (d. 1890)

BLOCK 8

Markham served as mayor of Atlanta in 1853 and later as the proprietor of the Markham House, one of Atlanta's finest post–Civil War hotels.

Thou hast gone to the hills of frankincense and myrrh until dawn breaketh and shadows fly away.

—Song of Solomon 4:6

JAMES A. WILLIAMSON, BLOCK 107

Samuel M. Inman (d. 1915)

BLOCK 8

Inman was a Confederate veteran and a partner with Joel Hurt in developing the Atlanta and Edgewood Street Railway as well as Inman Park, Atlanta's first planned suburb. His cotton business, S. M. Inman and Company, was once the state's largest. He was referred to as "Atlanta's First Citizen" for his leadership and generosity. Also buried at Oakland are his father, Shadrach Inman; his uncle, Walker P. Inman; and his brother, Hugh T. Inman.

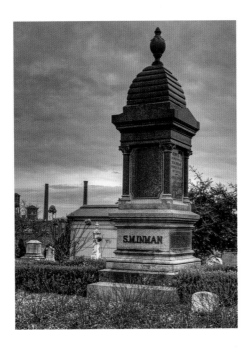

"Tell Eddie in Christ I place my trust."
"Papa wait at the head of the stair, I'm coming."

THE COMBINED EPITAPHS OF OLIVER BACON, WHO DIED ON MARCH 3, 1878, AND OF HIS SON, EDWIN, WHO DIED FIVE DAYS LATER, BLOCK 4

Rawson Mausoleum

BLOCK 30, BYZANTINE REVIVAL

William A. Rawson (d. 1879) was a local merchant and property owner. Also interred here are Charles Collier (d. 1900), Rawson's son-in-law and an Atlanta mayor, 1897-98; Collier's daughter Julia (d. 1967) and his son-in-law Julian Harris (d. 1963), the son of the writer Joel Chandler Harris. Julian and Julia Harris owned the *Columbus Enquirer-Sun* newspaper. They won the 1926 Pulitzer Prize on behalf of the paper for, according to the award citation, "the service which it rendered in its brave and energetic fight against the Ku Klux Klan; against the enactment of a law barring the teaching of evolution; against dishonest and incompetent public officials and for justice to the Negro and against lynching." Julia Harris was named a Georgia Woman of Achievement in 1998.

Dr. Daniel O'Keefe (d. 1871). A physician and member of Atlanta City Council, O'Keefe advocated for free public schools and has been called "the father of Atlanta Public Schools." (Block 62)

Henson-Parris Mausoleum (Classical Revival). Constructed in 1925. (Block 62)

Jett Rucker Vault (Eclectic). Rucker (d. 1900) was a forty-niner who participated in the California gold rush. He settled in Atlanta and was a banking partner of Robert Maddox and William Peel. (Block 14)

Murphy Mausoleum (Greek Revival). John E. Murphy (d. 1924) was a prominent Atlanta banker. His daughter, Julia, married Conkey Pate Whitehead, an heir to the Atlanta Coca-Cola Bottling Company fortune. Their onetime home, "Villa Juanita," still stands on West Paces Ferry Road next to the Georgia Governor's Mansion. (Block 82)

Dr. Nedom Angier (d. 1882). An early Atlanta settler, physician, druggist, educator, state treasurer, and mayor, 1877–78. (Block 13)

Russell Mitchell (d. 1905). A Confederate veteran and the paternal grandfather of Margaret Mitchell. (Block 22)

Sage Mausoleum (Greek Revival). Captain Ira Yale Sage (d. 1908) was a civil engineer whose firm built the Southern Railway's line from Charlotte to Birmingham. (Block 12)

Drs. Samuel Hape and Albert Hape. Samuel Hape (d. 1915) manufactured dental tools and supplies for the Confederate army. He was later a member of the Atlanta City Council and mayor of Hapeville, a small town close to his home that was named in his honor. His brother, Albert Hape (d. 1884), also a dentist, was a Confederate veteran wounded at the Battle of Griswoldville (Georgia). In 1869, he made the first balloon ascension over Atlanta. (Block 6)

Sanders-Hickey Mausoleum (Greek Revival). The structure was erected by William C. Sanders (d. 1900). (Block 55)

Swift-Burkhart-Dickey Mausoleum (Eclectic). Interred here is Maibelle Swift Dickey (d. 1977), the mother of the writer James Dickey, author of *Deliverance.* (Block 62)

Walters Mausoleum (Greek Revival). The building houses the remains of George Calhoun Walters (d. 1914) and his wife, Frances Winship Walters (d. 1954), the daughter of George Winship. (Block 87)

Gone Shopping.
KATHERINE TAYLOR, BLOCK 91

Confederate Memorial Grounds

THIS SECTION, the final resting place for approximately 6,900 Confederate soldiers, including 3,000 unknowns, truly reflects the words of Drew Gilpin Faust in *This Republic of Suffering*: "ordered row after row of humble identical markers, hundreds or thousands of men, known and unknown, who represented not so much the sorrow or particularity of a lost loved one as the enormous and all but unfathomable cost of war" (249).

Through much of the Civil War, Atlanta hospitals overflowed with men, both Union and Confederate, suffering from debilitating illnesses or wounded in battles to the north. The largest complex of wartime

hospitals in the area was along Fair Street (now Memorial Drive), within half a mile of the cemetery. As fighting moved closer to Atlanta and deaths mounted, land adjacent to the cemetery was acquired for use as additional burial grounds. After the war, several thousand soldiers who had fallen in the Atlanta campaign were moved from battlefield graves to Oakland.

As one approaches this area from the main gate, the Confederate Obelisk provides an orienting landmark, and marked military graves

occupy a large central rectangle south of the obelisk. Also here are the headstones of sixteen Union soldiers who died in local hospitals. Another area of marked Confederate graves lies along Oakland's southern wall. Northeast of the obelisk, the unmarked graves of the unknowns are guarded by the impressive *Lion of Atlanta*. The dying lion rests on the Confederate flag the soldiers followed and, in the words of a commemorative poem, "guards their dust." To the northwest of the obelisk are the graves of three Confederate generals: John Brown Gordon, Alfred Iverson Jr., and Clement Anselm Evans. Generals Lucius Gartrell and William Stephen Walker are interred at Oakland in family lots.

Notable Inhabitants and Structures

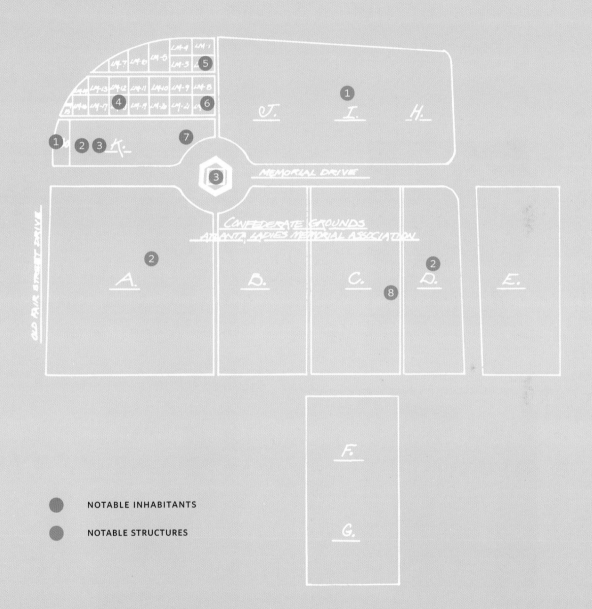

NOTABLE INHABITANTS

NOTABLE STRUCTURES

① Dr. Noel P. P. D'Alvigny (d. 1877)

BLOCK 130

Born in France in 1800, D'Alvigny served as a surgeon in the French army before coming to Atlanta in 1848. A founding faculty member of the Atlanta Medical College, he treated countless casualties in Atlanta hospitals during the Civil War. He is also credited with saving the college from being destroyed by Union troops in 1864. D'Alvigny may have been Margaret Mitchell's model for the character Dr. Meade in *Gone with the Wind*. He also cared for Dr. James Nissen, the first person buried at Oakland.

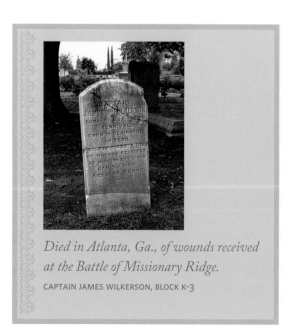

Died in Atlanta, Ga., of wounds received at the Battle of Missionary Ridge.

CAPTAIN JAMES WILKERSON, BLOCK K-3

② General John B. Gordon (d. 1904) and Fannie Haralson Gordon (d. 1931)

BLOCK K-3

Despite a lack of military education, Gordon rose to become a Confederate major general, serving under Robert E. Lee. After the war, he was elected U.S. senator and then Georgia governor (1886–90). Gordon's wife, Fannie Haralson Gordon, was a leader of the Atlanta Ladies Memorial Association (ALMA) and was instrumental in the relocation of Confederate dead from battlefield graves to the Confederate Memorial Grounds at Oakland.

General John B. Gordon, ca. 1860s

Dr. D'Alvigny's Deception

BORN IN FRANCE IN 1800, Dr. Noel P. P. D'Alvigny fought in the Battle of Waterloo at fifteen. He later served as a surgeon in the French army before immigrating to the United States. He came to Atlanta in 1848 to practice medicine, later serving on the faculty of the Atlanta Medical College, established in 1854. With the outbreak of the Civil War, the college closed and the school's building was converted for use as a hospital. During the bitter fighting in Georgia in 1863–64, D'Alvigny was nearly omnipresent, caring for the wounded and dying in hospitals across the city. In early September 1864, when Atlanta was surrounded and the Confederate forces were preparing to evacuate, D'Alvigny was placed in charge of the wounded soldiers housed in the medical college. In the following weeks, Union soldiers permitted the doctor to continue ministering to his patients unmolested. Eventually, nearly all the wounded were discharged or evacuated.

Atlanta Medical College, ca. 1860

Finally, as Union forces prepared to leave Atlanta in November, an order was issued for the burning of the city's commercial buildings, warehouses, and other structures—including the college. Determined to prevent the destruction of the school, D'Alvigny plied a number of hospital attendants with whiskey and placed them in an upstairs room with instructions to moan as if they were in pain. That evening, he arrived at the medical college to find Union soldiers breaking cots and beds for kindling in preparation for torching the building. He complained to an officer that "this was the first time that he had ever seen sick and wounded men burned without even giving them a chance for removal" (quoted in Garrett, *Atlanta and Environs*, 1:652). The officer vehemently denied that there were any wounded in the building. At that point, D'Alvigny threw open the doors to the upstairs room to show him the moaning attendants. Perplexed, the Union officer gave the doctor until daylight to remove the patients. But by dawn the Union army was on the march and the building was saved.

3 Brigadier General Alfred Iverson (d. 1911)

BLOCK K-4

The son of a U.S. senator, Iverson served in the Mexican War. In 1861, he joined the Confederate army, rising to the rank of brigadier general. In the 1864 Atlanta campaign, he commanded a cavalry brigade under General Joseph Wheeler.

> *Gently close his little eyes,*
> *And fold his dimpled hands,*
> *For with our little darling now,*
> *A white robed angel stands.*
>
> H. C. BEERMANN JR., BLOCK 20

4 William J. Northen (d. 1913)

BLOCK LM-18

Exempt from combat during the Civil War, Northen served in Atlanta and Macon hospitals. He was elected to the state legislature in 1877, the state senate in 1884, and the governorship in 1890. While governor, Northen collaborated with Philander Fitzgerald, a former Union army drummer boy and later a pension attorney and newspaper publisher, to establish the southern Georgia town of Fitzgerald as a warm-weather colony for aging Union veterans and their families. For many years, the town served as a model for the nation's reconciliation after the Civil War.

Governor William Northen, ca. 1890s

Governor William Northen in Fitzgerald, Georgia, for the dedication of the town, 1897

5 *Major Joseph Morgan (d. 1928) and Eugenia Goode Morgan (d. 1924)*

BLOCK LM-2

A Confederate veteran, Major Morgan drew up the plans for the Confederate Memorial Grounds and produced the first wooden headboards for the graves in 1866–67. Eugenia Goode Morgan was the first president of ALMA.

6 *Captain John Milledge (d. 1899) and Fannie C. Milledge (d. 1895)*

BLOCK LM-22

Milledge, a Confederate officer and lawyer, served for many years as the state librarian. He was the grandson of Governor John Milledge (1802–6), for whom Milledgeville was named. Fannie Milledge was an active leader of ALMA.

John Milledge, ca. 1870s

Fannie Milledge, ca. 1870s

7 *Brigadier General Clement Anselm Evans (d. 1911)*

BLOCK K-9

Evans was a division commander of infantry in the Army of Northern Virginia, serving under General Robert E. Lee. He led his troops in the last battle before the Confederate surrender at Appomattox Courthouse, Virginia, in 1865. After the war, Evans was ordained as a Methodist minister. He edited the twelve-volume *Confederate Military History* and served as president of the United Confederate Veterans.

General Clement A. Evans, 1898

① Lion of Atlanta

LION SQUARE

Sculpted by T. M. Brady, this monument was unveiled on Confederate Memorial Day 1894. The memorial, depicting a dying lion resting on a Confederate battle flag, was dedicated to the unknown dead interred in the surrounding square.

② Marble Monuments

SECTIONS A AND D

Placed in the Confederate Memorial Grounds in 1892, the two monuments record the names of several thousand Confederate soldiers interred at Oakland whose final resting places are unknown.

⑧ Union soldiers' graves

SECTION C-10

During the war, more than two thousand Union soldiers were treated in Atlanta's hospitals, and several hundred died and were buried at Oakland. After the war, nearly all were exhumed and returned to their home states or to the National Cemetery in Chattanooga. Today, there are sixteen Union graves still located at Oakland.

③ Confederate Monument (1874)

CONFEDERATE DRIVE

The cornerstone of the monumental Egyptian Revival–style obelisk was laid on October 15, 1870, and the monument was dedicated on Confederate Memorial Day 1874.

Other Significant Inhabitants and Structures

Croft—husband and wife markers. This is the only site in the Confederate soldiers' portion of the grounds where a husband and wife are interred together. Little is known of the circumstances surrounding the deaths of F. M. Croft or his wife. According to the gravestones, they died one day apart, April 18 and 19, 1864. (Section A-3-7)

Lucien Weakly. This family-placed marker is the final resting place of a young Confederate soldier mortally wounded in the Battle of Chickamauga in September 1863. The Historic Oakland archives refer to a letter written to Weakley's mother by one of Lucien's brothers who visited the grave in the 1870s and planted a magnolia seed behind his headstone. Today, the grave is dwarfed by a massive magnolia tree. (Section A-10-6)

E. Taylor barrel vault. When restored in the 1990s, this brick structure was determined to be a faux vault over a soldier's grave. (Section B-1-4)

Child Square, Jewish Flat, and Jewish Hill

Child Square

This land, acquired in the cemetery's 1857 expansion, is located on the east-facing slope between the Original Six Acres and the Jewish Flat. The origin of the name has been lost, but the space may have originally served as a final resting place for orphans and homeless children who died in antebellum Atlanta; however, there are not an unusually large number of children's graves in this section. Notable persons interred in Child Square include the famed golfer Robert Tyre "Bobby" Jones Jr. and Jeff Cain, the engineer of the locomotive "General," which was stolen in the Great Locomotive Chase in 1862.

Jewish Flat and Jewish Hill

In 1860, Atlanta was home to approximately fifty Jewish residents. They organized the Hebrew Benevolent Association (predecessor of the Hebrew Benevolent Congregation), and its president, David Mayer, arranged to purchase six burial lots at Oakland within the Original Six Acres. Now known as the Old Jewish Burial Grounds, this area along the southern

wall is one of the oldest Jewish burial grounds in Georgia. For several years, the bodies of Jewish residents of Atlanta, as well as those from communities across Georgia and adjoining states that lacked consecrated Jewish burial grounds, were brought here for interment.

After the Civil War, Atlanta's Jewish population continued to grow. In 1878, the Hebrew Benevolent Congregation (the Temple) acquired an additional ten lots in a lowland area, now called

Jewish Flat, along the southern wall and east of the Confederate section. In 1895, the Temple sold a parcel of the land to the recently established Avahath Achim Congregation, which was composed of recently arrived immigrants from Russia, Poland, and eastern Europe. This area is distinctive for its crowded, "forest-like" appearance with many tall, tightly spaced markers. This burial style may have reflected the need to maximize use of the space for those with limited financial resources. A year later, the Temple sold a parcel of land in the flat to the Kadish Lodge, a secular order of Russian Jews that provided free burial sites to its members.

At the same time, land on the hillside east of Jewish Flat was acquired for additional Jewish burials. The site, known as Jewish Hill, was a more desirable location and served as the final resting place for some of Atlanta's most prominent Jewish inhabitants of the nineteenth and early twentieth centuries.

Notable Inhabitants and Structures

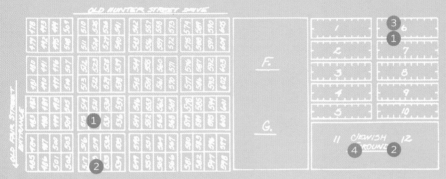

● **NOTABLE INHABITANTS**

● **NOTABLE STRUCTURES**

① *Jeff Cain (d. 1897)*

BLOCK 520

Cain was the engineer of the Western and Atlantic Railroad engine "General," which was stolen by Union raiders on April 12, 1862. Along with William Fuller and Anthony Murphy (both interred at Oakland), Cain was involved in the pursuit of the raiders in the Great Locomotive Chase.

> *A life so full Heaven had to wait. Gone fishing.*
>
> WILBURN "TENNESSEE" RYDER, WHO DIED AT AGE 100, BLOCK 489

② *Robert T. "Bobby" Jones Jr. (d. 1971)*

BLOCK 518

Jones, a native Atlantan, earned fame as an amateur golfer. He was considered the finest player of his day, winning the Grand Slam of golf in 1930 (U.S. Amateur and Open; British Amateur and Open). He retired from competitive play in 1930 to pursue his law career, but was instrumental in the establishment of the Augusta National Golf Club. Jones designed its famed course, now home to the Masters Tournament, which he cofounded in 1934. In 1958, St. Andrews, Scotland, home of the famed Old Course, where Jones won the 1930 British Amateur, named him a Freeman of the City. He was only the second American to be so honored, the first being Benjamin Franklin. Golfers often place golf balls on Jones's grave in tribute or for golfing good luck.

The golfer Bobby Jones with young Charles Harrison, ca. 1950s

③ ① Morris Hirsch Mausoleum

BLOCK J-6, ECLECTIC

Hirsch (d. 1906), with his brothers Joseph and
Henry, opened a clothing store in Atlanta in
1863. Hirsch's Clothing stores remained in
business for more than a century.

④ ② Ahavath Achim Section (1892) and Kadish Lodge Section (1895)

BLOCKS J-11, J-12, J-5

Purchased from the Temple by a congregation
composed of Russian, Polish, and eastern
European immigrants, this section of closely
spaced markers reflects both the burial
traditions and the modest means of Ahavath
Achim's members. In 1896, the Temple sold a
small parcel of land to Kadish Lodge of Brith
Abraham, a secular organization of Russian
Jews that provided its members with illness
benefits and burial space.

⑤ ③ Dr. Joseph Jacobs Mausoleum

BLOCK 269, BEAUX-ARTS CLASSICAL

A Georgia native, Jacobs (d. 1929) apprenticed
in Dr. Crawford Long's drugstore in Athens
before attending the Philadelphia College of
Pharmacy and Science. He later opened his own
shop at Five Points in Atlanta, where, in 1887,
Coca-Cola was first served as a fountain drink.
Jacobs's son, Sinclair Jacobs (d. 1977), served as
a pharmacist in the Emory Medical Unit in
France during World War I.

Dr. Joseph Jacobs: In the Right Place at the Right Time

BORN IN Jefferson, Georgia, in 1859, Joseph Jacobs moved with his family to Athens, Georgia, when he was a boy. This move would eventually bring him into contact with two of Georgia's and the nation's most illustrious figures. As a young teen, he apprenticed in the Broad Street apothecary shop and medical office owned by Dr. Crawford Long. Himself a Jefferson native born in 1815, Long studied medicine at Transylvania College and the University of Pennsylvania before returning to Jefferson to practice in the early 1840s. Familiar with the mind-numbing properties of ether, on March 31, 1842, Long persuaded a patient to inhale ether while he excised a tumor from his neck. The operation was successful, and the patient, James Venable, reported that he felt no pain from the experience. This experiment is now considered the first painless surgery, and Dr. Long is recognized around the world as the "father of anesthesia." After a brief stay in Atlanta, Long moved to Athens in the 1850s to practice medicine and operate a drugstore in partnership with his brother.

Jacobs Pharmacy at Five Points, ca. 1910

Joe Jacobs's work under Dr. Long's tutelage piqued his interest in the field, and he went on to study at the Philadelphia College of Pharmacy and Science. He returned to Athens in 1879 to open his own store, but moved to Atlanta five years later for its greater business opportunities. Jacobs purchased an old drugstore in downtown Atlanta's Five Points in 1884. Before his death in 1929, he owned a chain of sixteen stores throughout the city.

In the mid-1880s, Dr. John Pemberton was promoting the sale of a headache tonic he called Coca-Cola to local drugstores. According to Pemberton's instructions, the tonic's syrup needed to be mixed with water before being dispensed to buyers. In early 1887, a headache sufferer entered Jacobs Pharmacy at Five Points and ordered a dose of the tonic. The clerk, Willis Venable, mistakenly added carbonated water instead of tap water to the Coca-Cola syrup. The customer commented that it really tasted good, and the rest is retailing history.

6 4 *Regenstein Family Vault*

BLOCK 270, ECLECTIC

Julius Regenstein (d. 1914) and Gabriel Regenstein (d. 1897) came to Atlanta in 1872 to open a millinery store on Whitehall Street. The business became one of Atlanta's most popular clothing stores for more than a century. Regenstein's was reputed to have become the first retailer in the South to employ a female clerk when Julius offered a job to a Confederate soldier's widow.

7 *Rich Family Lot*

BLOCK 277

Morris Rich (d. 1928) immigrated to America in 1859 and arrived in Atlanta in 1867. He borrowed $500 from his brother William to open M. Rich Dry Goods. His brothers Daniel and Emanuel (d. 1897) joined the business in 1871. Rich's went on to become one of one of Atlanta's and the region's most prosperous retailers. In 1924, Rich built a large store on Broad and Alabama Streets that remains an Atlanta landmark (it is now part of a federal office complex). Members of the Rich family were generous philanthropists, even agreeing to cash vouchers that the city issued to schoolteachers when it was too poor to pay them during the Depression.

Morris Rich, ca. 1920s

⑧ ⑤ *Elsas Family Mausoleum*
BLOCK 278, ECLECTIC

Jacob Elsas (d. 1932) emigrated from Germany to America in the 1850s and was a soldier in General Sherman's invading army in 1864. At war's end, he returned to Georgia, opening a store in Cartersville. He moved to Atlanta in 1869 and started a dry goods and clothing shop. After finding it difficult to secure a steady supply of paper and cloth bags for his merchandise, he built the Fulton Bag and Cotton Mill, one of the city's first cotton mills, on the site of the former Atlanta Rolling Mill. Elsas was involved in the founding of Georgia Tech and made the first contribution to erect a hospital to honor the memory of his friend Henry Grady.

Jacob Elsas, ca. 1920s

⑨ *Haas Family Lot*
BLOCK 276

Jacob Haas came south from Philadelphia and settled in Marthasville in 1845. He was reputed to have been the town's first Jewish citizen. His daughter Caroline (d. 1910) was born in Atlanta in 1848. Haas returned to Philadelphia in 1851, leaving his dry-goods business to David Mayer (later president of the Hebrew Benevolent Association). Haas died there in 1855, and his widow, Jeannette, returned to Atlanta. When Caroline married, her husband was also named Jacob Haas (d. 1909), possibly a relative of her father. The elder Haas's brother, Herman (d. 1884), came to Atlanta in 1848. His son, Aaron Haas (d. 1912), was a Confederate veteran and former blockade runner. He was a railroad executive and founding partner of the real estate and insurance company Haas and Howell.

> *Beloved, having dragged the net about us, And knitted mesh to mesh, we grow immortal.*
>
> —William Butler Yeats, "The Shadowy Waters"
> CHESTER WAYNE HARRIS, BLOCK 493

Other Significant Inhabitants and Structures

David Zaban (d. 1921). Zaban was an early president of Ahavath Achim Congregation. The Marcus Jewish Community Center's Zaban Park is named for his family. (Section J-12-17)

Selig family. Emil Selig (d. 1914) was the son of Sigmund Selig, a pioneer Jewish settler in Atlanta. Emil's wife, Josephine Cohen Selig (d. 1933), was also from an early Atlanta Jewish family. Their daughter, Lucille (d. 1957), was married to Leo Frank, who was convicted for the 1913 murder of a young girl, Mary Phagan. His sentence was commuted in 1915 by Governor John Slaton, but an angry mob kidnapped him from the state prison and lynched him. The infamous case received national publicity and criticism. In the 1960s, family members interred Lucille's ashes beside her parents. (Block 279)

Rogers Hill

OCCUPYING THE southeastern corner of Oakland, this section rises to a ridge above Jewish Flat and Jewish Hill before gradually descending to Potters' Field and the eastern boundary wall at Boulevard and Memorial Drive. The land was part of an expansion of the cemetery through the 1867 purchase of property from Lemuel P. Grant, at the time one of Atlanta's largest landowners. A few blocks to the south of Oakland is Grant Park, a city park that is home to the

Atlanta Cyclorama and Zoo Atlanta. Lemuel Grant's home
near the park, undergoing restoration after years in disrepair, is
headquarters for the nonprofit Atlanta Preservation Center.

While the origin of the name
of the section is obscure, it may
have come from the location of
the graves of the John Henry
Rogers family on the western
slope of the hill.

In an interesting historical
footnote, Rogers Hill is the final
resting place of Clark Howell
(d. 1882), who built Howell's Mill
north of Atlanta in the 1850s.
He is interred only a short
distance from the site where a Confederate artillery battery set
up during the Battle of Atlanta. The battery commander was
Captain Evan P. Howell, Clark Howell's son.

Notable Inhabitants
and Structures

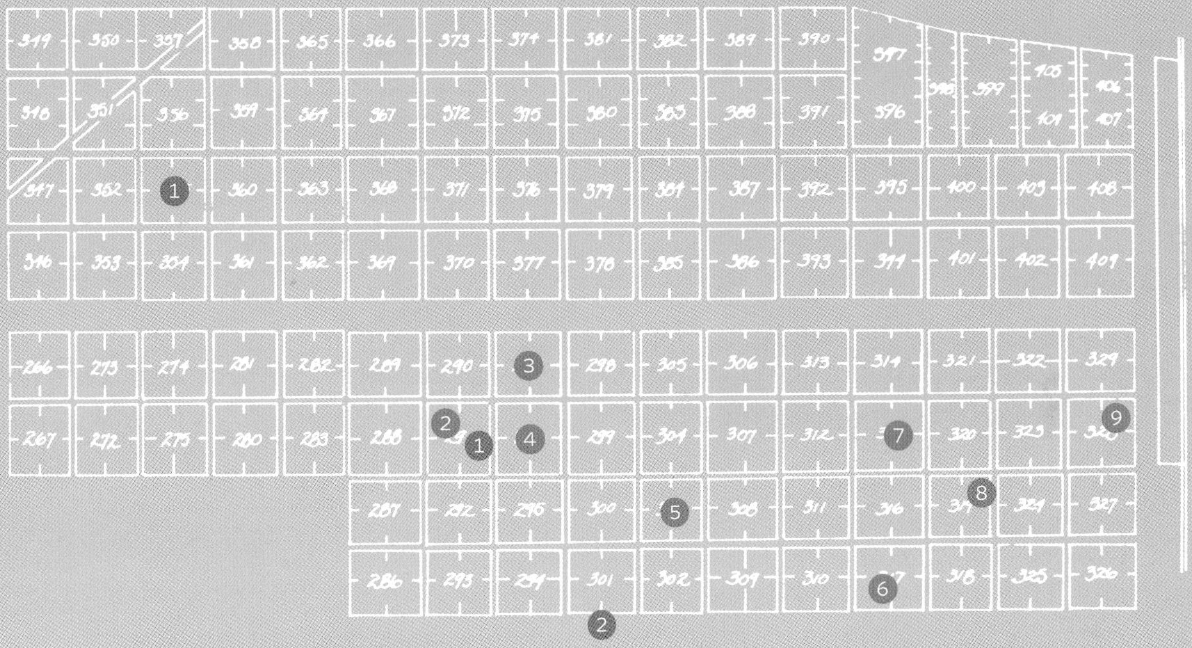

NOTABLE INHABITANTS

NOTABLE STRUCTURES

① Rogers Family Lot

BLOCK 355

John Henry Rogers (d. 1950) purchased this lot in 1884, possibly as a final resting place for his mother, Mary Rogers (d. 1884).

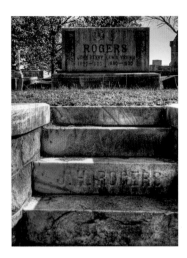

① Sawtell Mausoleum

BLOCK 291, ECLECTIC

Henry Clay Sawtell (d. 1907) purchased this lot in 1880 as a final resting place for his infant child. The mausoleum was erected before Sawtell's death.

② Bernard Mallon (d. 1879)

BLOCK 291

Born in Ireland in 1824, Mallon immigrated to New York City in 1827. He moved to Savannah, Georgia, in 1850 to teach in a private school. City leaders asked him to organize a system of public schools, and in 1856, he established the Massie School. He continued to teach during the Civil War, first in Savannah and later in Whitesville, where many Savannah families had fled. In 1864, he came to Atlanta with a militia unit to aid in the city's defense, but fell ill and returned to Savannah. He moved to Atlanta in 1871 to serve as the first superintendent of the city's public schools. In 1879, Mallon accepted an invitation from Texas authorities to organize that state's first normal school (teachers college). He moved to Huntsville, Texas, to become the first president of the Sam Houston Normal Institute (now Sam Houston State University), but died after only a few months in the office. His body was returned to Atlanta for burial at Oakland, and the funeral was one of the largest in the city up to that time.

3   *Hugh T. Inman Family Lot*

BLOCK 297

The son of the pioneer settler Shadrach Inman (d. 1896), who is also buried here, Hugh T. Inman (d. 1910) prospered in cotton brokerage and milling after the Civil War. He served multiple terms on the Atlanta City Council and was, at the time of his death, the wealthiest man in Georgia. Hugh Inman's son, Edward (d. 1931), buried here, commissioned the Atlanta architect Philip T. Shutze to design his elegant Buckhead home, "Swan House," completed in 1928. It is now part of the Atlanta History Center. Hugh's daughter, Anne, married John W. Grant, and is interred in the Grant family mausoleum. Especially poignant are the monuments to two of Hugh Inman's children: Hugh, who died at age two in 1881, and Louise, who died at age five in 1888. The effigies were sculpted to resemble the children.

4   *Ivan Allen Jr. (d. 2003) and Louise Allen (d. 2008)*

BLOCK 296

Born in Atlanta in 1911, Ivan Allen Jr. was active in business, civic, and community affairs for many years. He is best remembered for his two terms as mayor of Atlanta (1962–70), when he skillfully shepherded the city through the turbulent racial unrest of the 1960s and brought major-league sports to Atlanta. Ivan Allen's wife, Louise Richardson Allen, was the daughter of the real estate developer Hugh Richardson, and the granddaughter of Hugh T. Inman. She was a founding board member of the Historic Oakland Foundation and a longtime board member and benefactor of the Atlanta History Center.

Mayor Ivan Allen and Louise Allen, election night, 1961

Andrews' Raiders Historical Marker

BRICK WALL ACROSS FROM BLOCK 301

This marker notes the nearby site where seven Union soldiers, members of a raiding party that stole the locomotive "General" on April 12, 1862, were hanged as spies on June 18, 1862. Their bodies were interred at Oakland until 1866, when they were moved to the Chattanooga National Cemetery.

M. Hoke Smith (d. 1931)

BLOCK 303

Born in North Carolina in 1855, Smith moved to Atlanta with his family in 1868 when his father took a position in the Atlanta public schools. He read law and passed the bar exam in 1873 at age seventeen. Smith became one of Atlanta's most prominent attorneys and utilized his wealth to purchase the *Atlanta Journal* newspaper in 1887. He actively supported Grover Cleveland in the 1892 presidential campaign, and served as Cleveland's secretary of the interior (1893–96). He won the Georgia gubernatorial race in 1906, but lost a bid for reelection to Joseph M. Brown, the son of the Civil War governor Joseph E. Brown (both are buried at Oakland). He regained the office in 1910, but left it in 1911 to fill a vacant seat in the U.S. Senate. He served in Congress until 1920.

Gottfried Norrman (d. 1909)

BLOCK 317

Born in Sweden in 1846 and educated in Europe, Norrman came to Atlanta in 1881. He became one of the region's premier designers of Queen Anne–style residences and public buildings. Among Norrman's most notable Atlanta commissions were Ivy Hall in Midtown Atlanta for Edward Peters (1883) and Fountain Hall on the campus of Morris Brown College (1882).

Benjamin H. Hill (d. 1882)

BLOCK 315

Born in Georgia in 1823, Hill graduated from the University of Georgia and became a prosperous attorney in LaGrange, Georgia. He was elected to the state legislature in 1851, but lost his bid for reelection. In 1857, he ran for governor, losing to Joseph E. Brown. Following Abraham Lincoln's election in 1860, Hill opposed the Southern secessionist movement. Nonetheless, he served in the Confederate Senate (1861–65). During Reconstruction, he won election to the U.S. House in 1875, and then to the U.S. Senate in 1877, serving until his death. Hill was considered among Georgia's most eloquent orators and is especially well known for his 1874 eulogy of General Robert E. Lee. A statue of Senator Hill, originally located on Peachtree and Baker Streets, now stands in the Georgia State Capitol.

Benjamin H. Hill, ca. 1870s

Benjamin H. Hill and the New South

IN 1871, fifteen years before the journalist Henry Grady gave his renowned speech on the rise of a "New South" to an audience in New York City, Senator Benjamin H. Hill introduced the idea during his commencement address at the University of Georgia. Hill called on the young men (at the time the school was all-male) to cast aside the destructive ways of the slaveholding past and embrace education in the sciences, engineering, and technology as the path to the state's future.

Hill, a leading voice of moderation and opponent of secession, nonetheless served in the Confederate Senate throughout the Civil War, where he often supported President Jefferson Davis and opposed the actions of Georgia governor Joseph E. Brown. Following the South's defeat, Hill urged Georgians to accept Reconstruction as a fait accompli, a position that earned him many political enemies. Despite the efforts of his opponents, Hill was elected to Congress in 1875 and later to the U.S. Senate, serving there until his death in 1882.

During that 1871 graduation address in Athens, he called on the state to dramatically increase funding for its educational institutions if it wanted to compete with northern states in business, industry, and the sciences. In closing, he made a powerful statement that remains as true today as when he spoke: "There is nothing so costly as ignorance and nothing as cheap as knowledge."

8 *Brigadier General William S. Walker (d. 1899)*

BLOCK 319

Born in Pittsburgh, Pennsylvania, in 1822 and raised in Mississippi and Florida, Walker joined the army in 1845, serving with distinction in the Mexican War. He left the army in 1848, but rejoined in 1855 to command a company of cavalry. He resigned to enlist in the Confederate army in 1861, rising to the rank of brigadier general. He was severely wounded and captured at the Battle of Petersburg (in Virginia) in 1864. After being exchanged, he returned to service and surrendered with his troops in 1865.

9 *John Gray Westmoreland (d. 1887)*

BLOCK 328

Born in Jasper County, Georgia, in 1816, Westmoreland graduated from the Medical College of Georgia in 1843. He came to Atlanta with his younger brother, Willis F. Westmoreland, MD, in 1853. The two brothers led a group of local physicians, including Dr. Noel P. P. D'Alvigny, in establishing the Atlanta Medical College in 1854, with John serving as dean and Willis as professor of surgery. The first classes were held in City Hall before a permanent building was completed in 1855. When the school suspended operations in 1861, John Westmoreland converted it for use as a Confederate army hospital; he also served as city physician. Beyond his work in medicine, Westmoreland served in the state legislature, as a leader in civic affairs, and as a founding board member of ALMA.

John G. Westmoreland,
ca. 1860s

Other Significant Inhabitants and Structures

Clark Howell (d. 1882). Howell was the owner of Howell's Mill on Peachtree Creek, the site of bitter fighting during the Civil War Battle of Peachtree Creek. His son, Captain Evan P. Howell, commanded an artillery battery in the Confederate Army of Tennessee. During the Battle of Atlanta, that battery was located near what is now the Rogers Hill section of Oakland. (Block 306)

Eventide Old Ladies Home Lot. These lots at the eastern end of the section were set aside for residents of the old ladies home that stood in West End during the early twentieth century. Amos G. Rhodes, a furniture store owner, was a benefactor of the home. In 1974, the Eventide home merged with the Wesley Woods Center of Emory University. (Block 406)

Potters' Field

THE ORIGIN of the term "potters' field" is drawn from the Gospel of Matthew, chapter 27, which describes Judas's sorrow for his betrayal of Jesus: "Then Judas, which had betrayed Him, saw that he was condemned, repented himself, and brought again the thirty pieces of silver to the chief priests . . . and they took counsel, and bought with them the potters' field to bury strangers in." Referred to as either "potters' fields" or "paupers' fields," these spaces, frequently in the least desirable section of cemeteries, were often set aside for the poor, itinerant travelers, or those who died unknown; they have been a part of many public burial grounds for several centuries.

Oakland Cemetery's Potters' Field, located in the northeastern section of the cemetery, is a 5.7-acre open meadow acquired as part of the purchase of land from Lemuel P. Grant in 1866. It was set aside to provide additional space in the growing city for the burial of those without means to buy private lots. In addition, it provided a place for the reinterment of slaves and free blacks whose bodies were moved from the cemetery's more desirable locations so that those lots could be resold. The inviting green space is now the resting place for approximately 7,500 individuals, the vast majority being African Americans, interred there because they were either poor or dispossessed. There is but a single monument to commemorate their lives.

Today, Potters' Field's open spaces, which feature a view of the Atlanta skyline in the distance, is a popular gathering place for picnickers and sunbathers as well as those seeking a place for quiet contemplation. This seems very much in keeping with the cemetery developers' intentions that these grounds should be places to be enjoyed by the living.

Notable Inhabitants
and Structures

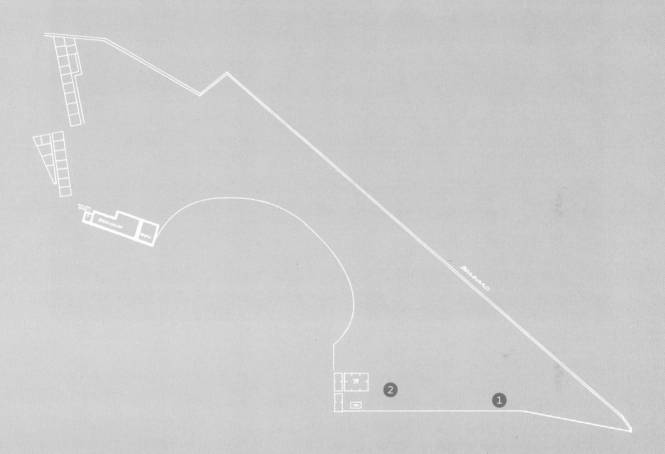

● NOTABLE STRUCTURES

① *Citizens Memorial*

MONUMENT ROAD ACROSS FROM ROGERS HILL

"A Memorial to the Citizens of Atlanta Who
Rest in Unmarked Graves," this monument
with bronze plaque is in the style of a false crypt
carved of granite. It was commissioned by an
anonymous donor in 1977.

② *Briggs Family Children's Marker*

NORTHEAST OF THE OLD COMFORT STATION

A simple tablet on a brick base memorializes
two Briggs children who died in 1881 and 1882.
The nearly illegible inscription notes that the
"grave was baught [*sic*] from the city."

What Lies Beneath?
Uncovering the Mysteries in Potters' Field

BENEATH THE CAREFULLY KEPT, tree-dotted lawn of Potters' Field lie thousands of untold stories from Atlanta's past. For many years, this open field along Oakland Cemetery's northeastern corner was believed to have been used exclusively for pauper burial of indigents and strangers, often with little ceremony or fanfare. Excavations of the area in the late 1970s changed this perception. In 1978, Historic Oakland Cemetery, Inc.,

commissioned Roy Dickens Jr., an archeologist, and Robert Blakely, a physical anthropologist, to conduct a cultural-resources investigation of Potters' Field. Questions to be answered included how many individuals are interred there and what is known about them. Assisted by anthropology students from Georgia State University, the researchers excavated thirteen trenches that revealed grave pits and a wide variety of artifacts from burials that were far from simple.

To reach the burial sites, it was necessary to dig through a layer of fill dirt believed to have been dumped on the site during construction of the nearby mill village of Cabbagetown in the 1880s. Embedded in this soil were numerous Civil War–era bullets, unfired artillery shells, and other debris, likely from the explosion nearby of the Confederate ammunition trains on September 1, 1864.

While the unearthing of household items and debris provided insight into the mill workers' daily lives, the unexpected discovery of quartz flakes and other objects near the African American Grounds suggested that the site may have been occupied by Paleo-Indians of the Old Quartz Culture more than six thousand years ago.

The graves themselves also told a surprising story. A significant number contained evidence of funerary offerings and objects, as well as remnants of clothing and jewelry, that told a very different story about the inhabitants of Potters' Field. In their summary report, the researchers noted: "Not all interred individuals were derived from Atlanta's pauper population. . . . Perhaps a sizeable portion . . . represents moderate-to-low income of Atlanta's Nineteenth century society." They went on to conclude: "It would be more accurate to view it as a segregated burial ground for Black Atlantans from a time when 'Black' and 'pauper' . . . may have been regarded as synonymous" (Dickens and Blakely, "Archeological Investigation in Oakland Cemetery," 310).

Under those green fields there is much more than meets the eye.

African American Grounds

SHORTLY AFTER Oakland Cemetery's establishment in 1850, the Atlanta City Council ordered the interment of slaves and free blacks to take place in "Slave Square," a segregated and less desirable parcel of ground at the far eastern end of the six-acre graveyard. Records of pre–Civil War burials often contain more information about the slave owner than the deceased slave. An example was the first documented black interment, a fourteen-year-old boy named John, buried February 10, 1853.

The name of the slaveholder, William Hearing, is listed on the record in the space provided for John's surname.

With acquisition of the remaining acreage at Oakland in 1866 and 1867, Slave Square was nearer the center of the cemetery, making it a more highly desirable burial space. To accommodate white families, the remains of those interred there were exhumed and relocated farther east to the "colored pauper grounds" (Potters' Field). Later, a portion of the cemetery was set aside as the "colored section," where blacks could purchase private lots for interments. This space constitutes what is now referred to as the African American Grounds.

In the mid- to late nineteenth century, burial customs were often patterned on African traditions. Few could afford inscribed grave markers, choosing instead to use "natural markers" such as stones, trees, plants, or household objects. In Marilyn Yalom's book *The American Resting Place*, she notes: "Another practice is to leave a personal object belonging to the deceased on the grave, often the last one he or she touched" (35). As a result, the African American Grounds may appear to be largely unused, when, in fact, it is estimated that as many as twelve thousand people were buried within its boundaries.

Working within the color line established by the white majority in the aftermath of the Civil War, a number of the black Atlantans buried in this section are notable for the remarkable contributions they made in business, education, social service, religion, and other areas. Many others buried here lived far humbler lives. For some, a burial plot was the only property they ever owned.

For visitors, the African American Grounds remain a tangible link to a distant time of racial segregation and discrimination. Emblematic of the dramatic transformation brought about through the tireless efforts of Dr. Martin Luther King Jr., an Atlanta native, in the 1950s and 1960s, is the fact that the best-known African American buried at Oakland, Maynard H. Jackson, is not interred here but in the Original Six Acres' North Public Ground, not far from the Main Gate, where he faces the modern international city he was so instrumental in creating.

(A cell phone tour of the African American Grounds has been developed, and visitors may listen to details at designated tour stops. Information is available in the visitor center.)

Notable Inhabitants
and Structures

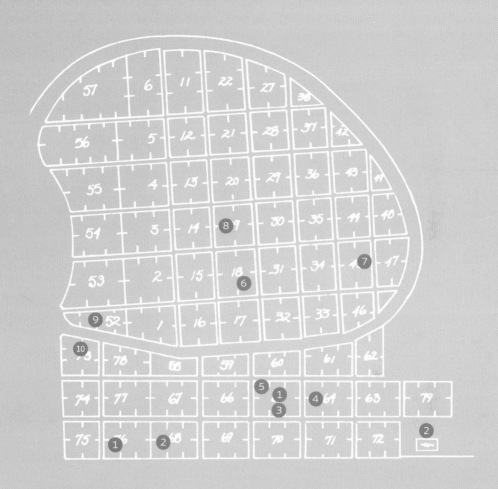

● NOTABLE INHABITANTS

● NOTABLE STRUCTURES

① *Dr. Thomas Slater (d. 1952)*

BLOCK 76

One of Atlanta's first black physicians and druggists, Slater was a medical partner of Dr. Henry R. Butler (buried nearby). Drs. Slater and Butler were founding members of the National Association of Colored Physicians, Dentists, and Pharmacists, the predecessor of the National Medical Association.

> Beneath the sod in sweet repose
> Is laid a mother's dearest pride
> A flower that scarce had waked to life
> And light and beauty ere it died.
> LEROY LAWRENCE, BLOCK 69

② *Dr. Henry R. Butler (d. 1931) and Selena Sloan Butler (d. 1964)*

BLOCK 68

Born a slave in 1862, Dr. Butler was Dr. Thomas Slater's medical partner and co-owner of the Gate City Drugstore, Atlanta's first black-owned pharmacy. Selena Sloan Butler was an 1888 Spelman Seminary graduate, educator, and founder of the National Congress of Colored Parents and Teachers Associations. In 1970, she was recognized as a founder of the National PTA. Selena Sloan Butler was recognized as a Georgia Woman of Achievement in 1995, and her portrait hangs in the State Capitol.

Selena Sloan Butler, ca. 1950s

Carrie Steele Logan: "She Hath Done All She Could"

ORPHANED AS A CHILD, Carrie Steele was born a slave on a Georgia plantation in 1829, yet learned to read and write. After the Civil War, she worked for a time as a matron in the Macon railroad station. Steele later moved to Atlanta, accepting a position at Union Station as a "stewardess" for the Central of Georgia Railroad, a position she held for twenty years. During those years, she grew increasingly concerned for Atlanta's many homeless African American children. Steele requested and received permission to use an abandoned boxcar as a shelter for children during the day so she could keep an eye on them. In the evening, several stayed in her small cottage on Wheat Street (Auburn Avenue); however, the number of children in her care soon exceeded the size of the home.

Carrie Steele Logan, ca. 1880s

To raise funds for a larger home, she resigned from the railroad in order to write and sell her autobiography. Steele also sold her home and solicited financial support from organizations and individuals across Atlanta. With the proceeds, she acquired a two-room house and opened the Carrie Steele Orphan Home in 1888. At the same time, she met and married the Reverend Josihia Logan, a minister from New York, who eagerly embraced her caring work.

In 1892, she opened a three-story home that could hold fifty children. In a gesture of support for her remarkable work, Atlanta mayor William Hemphill and the city council granted her a ninety-nine-year lease on her property. Beyond simply housing the orphans, the home provided a basic education, religious instruction, and technical training to aid the residents in finding employment.

Carrie Steele Logan directed the home until her death in 1900. She was succeeded by her longtime assistant, Clara Pitts, who guided the home for another forty years before handing the reins to her daughter Mae Maxwell Yates. On Yates's retirement in 1976, Olivette Allison, a former resident and later a social worker, directed the home until her death in 2010. Allison is interred at Oakland next to the Logan graves, and her monument features a bas-relief sculpture depicting the strong maternal bond between a mother and baby elephant.

It is estimated that over the last 120 years, the Carrie Steele–Pitts Home has housed more than twenty thousand children, providing love and care for some of the most disadvantaged youth in American society. Carrie Steele Logan's epitaph tells it all, stating simply, "Mother of Children, She Hath Done All She Could."

③ ① *Antoine Graves Mausoleum*

BLOCK 65, ECLECTIC

Graves (d. 1941) began his career as a teacher, and was principal of the Gate City School from 1884 to 1886. He went on to become one of Atlanta's most successful black real estate brokers. Graves's tomb is the sole mausoleum on the African American Grounds.

Antoine Graves, 1940

④ *Carrie Steele Logan (d. 1900) and the Reverend Josihia Logan (d. 1904)*

BLOCK 64

Despite being born a slave in 1829, Carrie Steele learned to read and write. After the Civil War, she spent sixteen years as a matron at the Macon railroad depot before moving to Atlanta for a similar job at Union Station. Concern about the plight of homeless black children prompted her to establish the Carrie Steele Logan Orphan Home in 1888 to care for them. Steele's husband, the Reverend Josihia Logan, a partner in her work, is buried beside her. Carrie Steele Logan was named a Georgia Woman of Achievement in 1998.

Ladies Comfort Station (1908)

[CLOSED]   EAST END OF SECTION ACROSS FROM
ROGERS HILL

One of two comfort stations erected for the cemetery's white visitors in the early 1900s, this structure was badly damaged in the 2008 tornado.

Bishop Wesley John Gaines (d. 1912)

BLOCK 65

The second pastor of Big Bethel AME Church, Gaines was born a slave in 1840. Frail and bedridden as a child, he secretly taught himself to read and write. Ordained a minister in 1867, he was elected a bishop of the African Methodist Episcopal (AME) Church in 1885. In 1891, he was instrumental in founding Morris Brown College.

Wesley John Gaines, ca. 1880s

James Tate Sr. (d. 1897)

BLOCK 18

Called the "father of black business in Atlanta," Tate opened the first black-owned business, a grocery store, in the post–Civil War city— with six dollars worth of merchandise. He also established the city's first school for black students, located in an abandoned boxcar. Tate was active in Republican Party politics and ran unsuccessfully for the state legislature.

Henry A. Rucker (d. 1924)

BLOCK 45

The president of the Georgia Real Estate Loan and Trust Co., Rucker was appointed by President William McKinley to serve as collector of internal revenue for Atlanta in 1897. The Rucker Building, at the corner of Piedmont and Auburn Avenues, was the first office building in Atlanta constructed for black professionals. It was demolished in 2001.

Henry Rucker, ca. 1900s

The Reverend Frank Quarles (d. 1881)
BLOCK 19 (SITE UNMARKED)

Quarles was the founding pastor of Friendship Baptist Church in 1866, Atlanta's oldest independent black congregation. He was instrumental in the establishment of Spelman and Morehouse Colleges.

Frank Quarles, ca. 1870s

Dr. Roderick Badger (d. 1890)
BLOCK 5

As a young slave in DeKalb County, Roderick was taught dentistry by his master, a white dentist, who was also his father. Badger opened a dental office in Atlanta in 1856 while still a slave, and then continued it as a free man. He built a successful practice that provided dental care to both black and white patients, much to the consternation of many local dentists of the day.

William Finch (d. 1917)
BLOCK 73

A former slave and a tailor by trade, Finch became the first black elected to the Atlanta City Council, in 1870. After he completed his one-year term, eighty-two years passed before another African American was elected to the city council. Finch was an advocate for public schools for black children and the employment of black teachers.

Other Significant Inhabitants and Structures

Augustus Thompson (d. 1910). The anvil atop Thompson's monument attests to his occupation as a blacksmith. The rings symbol reflects his membership in the Order of Odd Fellows. (Block 60)

Daughtery Hutchins (d. 1888). Born a slave, Hutchins opened a barbershop in Atlanta after the Civil War. He gave another ex-slave, Alonzo Herndon, his first job, and later made him his business partner. Herndon would go on to found the Atlanta Life Insurance Company and become one of the wealthiest blacks in the nation. (Block 4)

Malcolm Claiborne (d. 1870). Claiborne was among the blacks elected to the Georgia legislature in 1868. White legislators who disputed the elections were successful in expelling the thirty-three black representatives. Today, a sculpture on the grounds of the State Capitol commemorates the legislators "expelled because of their color." Two years later, Claiborne was shot by Moses Bently, the messenger of the House, during a dispute. (Exact burial site unknown)

Marie Woolfork Taylor (d. 1960). As a student at Howard University in 1908, Taylor helped found Alpha Kappa Alpha, the nation's first Greek-letter sorority for African American women. She was active in civic affairs and a board member of the Carrie Steele–Pitts Home. (Block 52)

Ransom Montgomery (d. 1883). Montgomery was a slave when he saved the passengers aboard a train bound for a burning bridge across the Chattahoochee. He was purchased from his owner by the state and given a parcel of land for his heroism. (Exact burial site unknown)

Hogpen Corner and Greenhouse Valley

THIS SECTION is composed of two
adjacent areas along the eastward-sloping
hills of the cemetery's northern quadrant.

Hogpen Corner

The name of this section serves as a
reminder that this area was, in the years
following Oakland's establishment,
farmland beyond Atlanta's town limits and
outside the cemetery's boundary. It also
indicates that Atlanta was still a small

town at that time, with rural spaces less than a mile from the zero milepost at the city's center. The land was purchased in 1866 from Lewis Schofield, the former owner of the Atlanta Rolling Mill, as the city began its rebuilding following the Civil War's devastation.

Hogpen Corner is south of the railroad tracks laid down by the Georgia Railroad in the 1840s. Much of the stone used in Oakland's many ornate mausoleums and large monuments was brought to the cemetery by these rails; in some instances, a temporary spur track was laid to the grave site for delivery of large or heavy materials. The section's proximity to the railroad may have made it a less desirable location, and as a result, there are few elaborate monuments and mausoleums here. One notable structure is the mausoleum of John C. Peck.

Greenhouse Valley

Composed of portions of the property acquired from Lewis Schofield and Lemuel P. Grant in 1866, Greenhouse Valley draws its name from

its proximity to the Oakland's second greenhouse, constructed in 1899. The cemetery established the first greenhouse in Atlanta in 1870, underscoring the garden heritage that has influenced Oakland for much of its existence. Plants and flowers were grown and preserved in the building until the 1890s. It was replaced by the current structure as part of the improvements that included erection of the new sexton's office and reception building. The adjacent maintenance barn and stables, also constructed in the late 1890s, now serve as storage areas for landscaping equipment and supplies.

Notable Inhabitants
and Structures

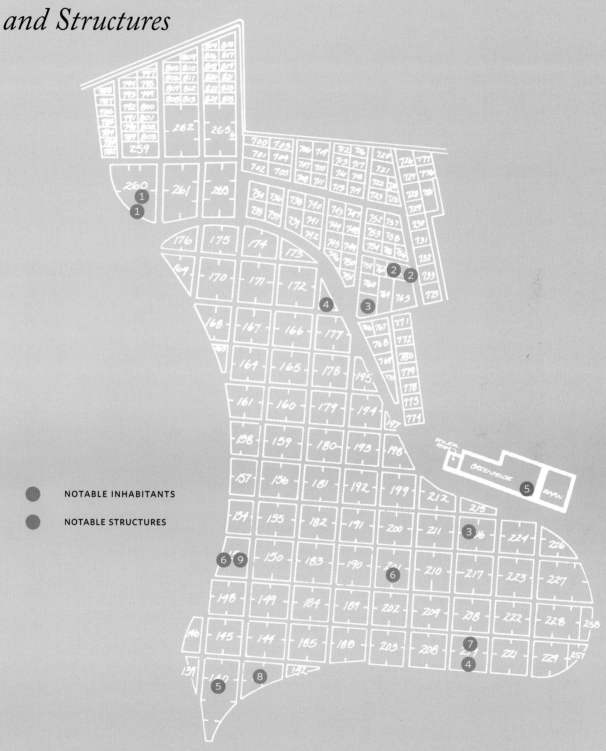

NOTABLE INHABITANTS

NOTABLE STRUCTURES

① ❶ John Calvin Peck Mausoleum

BLOCK 260, ECLECTIC

A native of Connecticut, Peck (d. 1906) moved to Atlanta in the 1850s to work as a building contractor. During the Civil War, his company produced thousands of sharpened wooden poles, dubbed "Joe Brown's Pikes" (named for the Civil War governor Joseph E. Brown, also buried at Oakland) as defensive weapons for the state militia.

She burned her candle at both ends,
but it made a lovely light.
—Adapted from Edna St. Vincent Millay,
"First Fig"
JULIA Z. BOWERS

He was a fool, but Julia loved him.
ALTON BOWERS, HUSBAND OF JULIA Z. BOWERS
(BOTH IN BLOCK 194)

② ❷ Erastus Gould Mausoleum

BLOCK 763, ECLECTIC

Born in Oswego, New York, in 1822, Gould (d. 1896) made his fortune in banking in Minneapolis, Minnesota, and moved to Atlanta in 1886. The following year, he commissioned the construction of the Traders Banking Company building on Decatur Street. The seven-story structure is considered among Atlanta's first skyscrapers. Later known as the Gould Building, it was demolished in 1935. Gould's elegant Inman Park home at Edgewood and Elizabeth Streets was dubbed "Gould's Marble Palace." Interred with him are his daughter Lillian and his son-in-law Elmer Chapman.

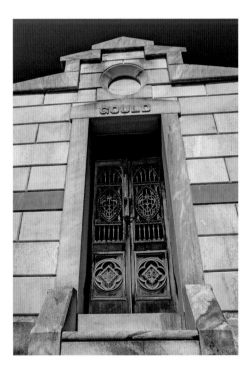

John Calvin Peck and the Mystery of Hardy Ivy's Grave

A MAUSOLEUM in Hogpen Corner near the northern border of the cemetery houses the earthly remains of John Calvin Peck, a native of Connecticut and a pioneer settler of Atlanta. Peck, who prospered as a general contractor, may be best known for manufacturing thousands of "Joe Brown's Pikes," dagger-tipped wooden poles produced at the order of Governor Joseph E. Brown to arm the state militia during the Civil War (there is no evidence that they were ever used in combat). After the war, Peck oversaw construction of the elegant Kimball House Hotel and, later, the erection of several buildings for the International Cotton Exposition (1881) and the Piedmont Exposition (1887).

In 1867, Peck began construction of his home near the intersection of Wheat Street (now Auburn Avenue) and Houston Street. This property was once owned by Hardy Ivy, the first white settler of what would become Atlanta. Following the removal of the Creek Indians in 1821, Ivy paid $225 for a 202.5-acre lot from DeKalb County in what is now downtown Atlanta. He built a crude cabin and farmed the land until his death from a riding accident in 1842. It was believed that his body was buried on his farm, but no records exist to confirm this. His wife, Sarah Todd Ivy, lived until 1865, and was buried in Oakland's Original Six Acres.

According to Peck family lore, tucked in a gated garden area at the back of the Peck home was a crude, unmarked stone marker. The Peck children and others always believed that this was Hardy Ivy's grave. In 1927, the Peck house was demolished to make way for future development, and the grave site was buried beneath ten feet of dirt. Consequently, the final resting place of Atlanta's first citizen may remain forever a mystery.

3 Fazzari–Landis Family Monument

BLOCK 761

A rare sculpture depicting a husband and wife seated together, this monument is a poignant memorial to Deborah Landis (d. 2006) by her husband Gerald Fazzari.

④ *Wooden Headboard*

TRIANGULAR BLOCK ACROSS FROM BLOCK 761

Nestled in the shade of a tree is the only known wooden headboard still in existence at Oakland. There is no legible information on the marker, and the identity of the person interred beneath is unknown.

⑤ *Oakland Greenhouse Complex (c. 1899)*

ACROSS FROM BLOCK 215

The three buildings include, *left to right*, a boiler room, Oakland's second greenhouse, and a barn. The greenhouse's glass roof deteriorated years ago, but the three structures remain in use as storage facilities for landscaping supplies and equipment.

③ *Isaac W. Avery (d. 1897)*

BLOCK 216

A former Confederate cavalry officer, Avery was a longtime editor of the *Atlanta Constitution*. He authored *The History of the State of Georgia from 1850 to 1881*, published in 1882.

⑥ *Winburn Monument*

BLOCK 201

The only Moderne style monument at Oakland, it holds the remains of William B. Winburn (d. 1919) and his wife, Nanie Belle Winburn (d. 1961).

④ ⑦ *James L. Dickey Sr. Mausoleum*

BLOCK 219, ECLECTIC

James Dickey Sr. (d. 1910) purchased a four hundred acre farm in Buckhead in 1903. After his death, the Tuxedo Park Company purchased land along West Paces Ferry Road from his estate and subdivided it for sale to wealthy Atlantans for the construction of elegant estates. James L. Dickey Jr. retained part of the land and commissioned the noted architect Neel Reid to design his home, "Arden," in 1917 on the site of his father's house. It still stands across from the former estate of his best friend, Robert F. Maddox (interred at Oakland), now the site of the Georgia Governor's Mansion.

⑧ Sawtell Rose Garden
BLOCK 141

A fragrant rose garden surrounds the Sawtell family lot and serves as a memorial to Alice Greene Sawtell (d. 1995), who enjoyed playing in Oakland Cemetery as a child in the early 1900s.

⑤ Boyd Family Lot, including Georgia Harris (d. 1920)
BLOCK 140

Interred here are the Confederate veteran Captain Isaac Boyd (d. 1904); his wife, Nannie S. Boyd (d. 1955), a founder of the Atlanta Art Association (predecessor of the High Museum); and their servant and former slave Georgia Harris. At the time of her death, the Boyd family petitioned Mayor James L. Key for permission to bury their "Negro Servant" in the part of the cemetery that was at that time reserved only for whites.

Tis hard to break the tender cord when love has bound the heart, tis hard, so hard to speak the words, we must forever part. Dearest love one, we have laid thee in the peaceful grave's embrace, but the memory will be cherished, till we see thy heavenly face.

—Popular memorial verse, author unknown

JOHN T. COOPER, BLOCK 145

⑥ ⑨ Clyde L. King Family Lot
BLOCK 151

King (d. 1941) purchased the Atlanta Plow Company in 1901, renamed it King Plow, and built it into one of the South's largest manufacturers of farm implements. After closing in 1986, the old factory was adapted for use as an award-winning arts center. With his wealth, King commissioned an elegant mansion in Druid Hills, which was completed in 1911. He and his wife, Clara, so loved the home that he had the design of its façade duplicated in this unusual burial monument.

Joy cometh in the morning.

—Psalms 30:5

GRACE WADDELL, BLOCK 140

Other Significant Inhabitants and Structures

Clarence Stephens (d. 1898). A nephew of Alexander H.
Stephens, he was the sexton of Oakland Cemetery when
he died. (Block 728)

Jonathan Norcross (d. 1898). A merchant, sawmill operator,
and owner of the *Atlanta Intelligencer* newspaper, Norcross
arrived in Marthasville in 1844. He lost the first mayoral
election to Moses Fornwalt, but became Atlanta's fourth
mayor, in 1851. He is the namesake of the city of Norcross,
Georgia. (Block 140)

Four

A Gathering Place

Oakland Cemetery's Vital Role in the Atlanta Community

In the absence of public gardens, rural cemeteries in a certain degree, supplied their place.
ANDREW JACKSON DOWNING,
Rural Essays

View of the cemetery from the Bell Tower

FOR SOME, the sight of picnickers lounging in the sun, a clown amusing children, a band performing, or strolling tourists may seem out of place in a graveyard. But those who designed Oakland Cemetery and other rural garden cemeteries recognized that these grounds were as important for the well-being of the living as they were for preserving the memory of the dead.

A little more than two centuries ago, graveyards were forbidding sites to be shunned as places of pestilential disease, foul odors, and tortured spirits. Doug Keister, the author of *Forever Dixie: A Field Guide to Southern Cemeteries and Their Residents*, described these grounds as "often little more than garbage dumps with a few haphazard wooden grave markers."[1] The result was a funerary landscape that may have served as a reminder of the grimness of death but offered little solace for those left behind.

During the nineteenth century, prevailing attitudes toward death and dying changed notably. The austerity and stoicism of earlier years were gradually replaced by a more romanticized view of death as "blessed sleep," a time of rest from the labors and trials of life and of anticipation of reunification in heaven. The fetid burial grounds of former times were replaced by rural garden cemeteries, first in Europe and later in the United States. Keister noted that this new style of burial ground was "modeled on English estate landscape design and was intended to provide a more bucolic environment for tending the dead."[2]

In a 1976 article written for *Monument Builder News*, Eileen Mueller noted that the garden cemeteries developed by nature-loving Victorians featured "great vistas of lawn, groves of trees, luxuriant flower beds . . . all intertwined with carefully placed walks and carriage drives."[3] The stark graveyards of colonial America were slowly supplanted by burial parks that would become destinations for Sunday drives, casual strolls, and even picnics. Mueller continued, "This enjoyment of the cemetery stemmed quite naturally from the Victorian's romantic attachment to death and his fondness for nature in a graveyard setting."[4] In keeping with this change in the prevailing view of death, simple gravestones gave way to more elaborate markers, monuments, and grand mausoleums that freely exhibited both secular and religious symbolism intended to convey messages from the dead to the living.

By the last quarter of the nineteenth century, Oakland Cemetery, like many cemeteries across the United States, was serving a dual function as both a burial ground and a community garden park. At the time, Atlanta, like many American cities, had few public parks, so the cemetery became a warm-weather gathering place for more than funerals and memorial events. An 1881 editorial in the *Atlanta Constitution* noted that Oakland, "in the absence of a public park, is quite popular with those of our citizens who enjoy a pleasant stroll."[5]

Confederate Memorial Day commemoration, ca. 1870s

But within a few decades, the development of public recreational parks and the introduction of the automobile offered people greater leisure alternatives both within the city and beyond. As visitation decreased, the cemetery entered a period of steady decline, nearly reverting to the forbidding landscape of earlier generations. Although Oakland was a city property, the individual lots were privately owned. Over the years, many lots were abandoned or forgotten by families, gravestones deteriorated, and lots became overgrown with weeds, severely taxing the city parks department staff responsible for the burial ground's basic maintenance.

The upcoming national bicentennial celebration in 1976 refocused attention on Oakland's condition. The cemetery became the second Georgia burial ground named to the National Register of Historic Places (the other was Bonaventure Cemetery in Savannah),

Confederate Memorial Day gathering, ca. 1901

prompting concerned Atlantans to form nonprofit Historic Oakland Cemetery, Inc., (now the Historic Oakland Foundation) to raise both community awareness of the cemetery's plight and funds for its stabilization, restoration, and preservation.

To achieve these objectives, the group sought increasingly creative ways to promote Oakland to a new generation of potential visitors. While the Atlanta Ladies Memorial Association and, later, the United Daughters of the Confederacy have sponsored an annual commemoration of Confederate Memorial Day at Oakland each April since 1866, foundation volunteers working with the City of Atlanta and like-minded groups from the Atlanta Historical Society (now the Atlanta History Center), the Atlanta Preservation Center, the Atlanta Junior League, and the Georgia Trust for Historic Preservation began planning a variety of other events to be held within the cemetery. Similar volunteer-led private initiatives were undertaken during this same period to preserve and restore other local public places that had suffered neglect from

Bird's-eye-view map of Atlanta, 1892

declining public funds for preservation and maintenance. Among these groups were the Piedmont Park Conservancy, the Grant Park Conservancy, and Friends of Zoo Atlanta.

Oakland's inaugural Sunday in the Park birthday celebration took place in 1977, followed in 1981 by the first Halloween candlelight tours, held in collaboration with the History Center. While the initial events drew modest crowds, each now welcomes thousands of participants each year.

Word spread of Oakland's appealing green spaces, remarkable funerary art and architecture, and tangible links to Atlanta's history. Visitation increased, and an expanding cadre of dedicated volunteers offered a variety of walking tours and events, including fun runs, photography workshops, music

Historic Oakland Cemetery, Inc.
and
The Bureau of Parks and Recreation
invite you to

OAKLAND CEMETERY'S 128TH
ANNIVERSARY CELEBRATION

on Sunday, September 24, 1978, from 2–5 P.M.
speakers   refreshments   music

In order to preserve the atmosphere of the 19th century cemetery and for your safety and enjoyment, we ask that you park outside the gates.

Oakland Cemetery birthday announcement, 1978

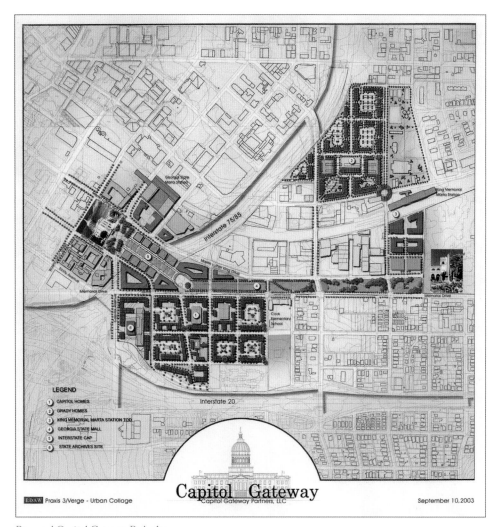

LEGEND
1 CAPITOL HOMES
2 GRADY HOMES
3 KING MEMORIAL MARTA STATION TOD
4 GEORGIA STATE MALL
5 INTERSTATE CAP
6 STATE ARCHIVES SITE

EDAW Praxis 3/Verge - Urban Collage

Capitol Gateway
Capitol Gateway Partners, LLC

September 10, 2003

Proposed Capitol Gateway Park plan

festivals, exhibitions, and lectures. In addition, the area around Oakland, from Cabbagetown to Grant Park and along Memorial Drive, underwent a renaissance, bringing a new generation of people to the neighborhoods. This, along with the development of a linear park linking the cemetery to the Georgia State Capitol grounds and downtown Atlanta—and a series of BeltLine parks along abandoned railways encircling the city—places Oakland in the heart of a vital and growing community.

Today, Oakland has regained its role as a gathering place for those seeking the enjoyment of an urban park, quiet spaces for meditation, and, of course, the opportunity to commune with the spirits of those who have gone before.

Volunteer Dan Childs portraying Governor John Slaton during a Halloween tour, 2010

Volunteer LaDorias Bias-Davis telling Georgia Harris's story during a Halloween tour, 2010

Volunteer Rob Merrick portraying Thomas Neal during a Halloween tour, 2010

Audience members captivated by the characters during a Halloween Tour, 2010

Children crossing the starting line in the
Run Like Heck fun run, 2010

Runners crossing the starting line in the
Run Like Hell race, 2010

The Seed and Feed Marching Band performing
before the Run Like Hell race, 2010

"Run Like Hell" T-shirts, 2010

Children chasing bubbles during Sunday in the Park, 2010

Ruby the Clown, a fixture at
Sunday in the Park, 2010

Cathy Kaemmerlen captivating
children with her storytelling during
Sunday in the Park, 2010

"Eternal love" in the
back of a classic Cadillac
during Sunday in the
Park, 2010

Visitors in Victorian garb for
Sunday in the Park, 2010

Harmony Express, one of the performing groups at
Sunday in the Park, 2010

Stephanie Parker shares tales during
Sunday in the Park, 2010.

The Bow Weevils performing at
Sunday in the Park, 2010

Preparations for a funeral at Oakland, 2010

Appendix A

Funerary Symbols Found at Oakland Cemetery

VISITORS TO OAKLAND may find nearly all of the following symbols during a walk through the grounds. The popularity of certain symbols has changed over time, so their prevalence or absence in a particular section may serve as a general chronological marker for succeeding eras of interment. Many monuments contain multiple symbols, indicating that there are many facets to the story being told in the stone. An excellent resource for learning more about funerary symbolism is *Stories in Stone: A Field Guide to Cemetery Symbolism and Iconography*, by Douglas Keister.

ALL-SEEING EYE. Often accompanied by rays of light, this symbolized the omniscience of God; also seen as a Masonic symbol.

All-seeing eye, Knit Mill

ANCHOR. Representing hope and faith. It may also be seen on the graves of seamen as evidence of their occupation.

ANCHOR AND CROSS. An early Christian symbol of Christ.

Anchor and cross, Child Square

ANGELS AND CHERUBS. Angels, the messengers of God, represent spirituality and the protection of the deceased.

Angel on the Jones family monument, Knit Mill

BED OR COUCH. Reflects the Victorian view of death as "blessed sleep." Pillows occasionally were included to complete the symbolism.

BIBLE. Whether depicted opened or closed, the Bible represents a belief in resurrection through the Scripture. It may also signify that the departed was a member of the clergy.

BIRD. A symbol of eternal life.

Dove. In both Christian and Jewish faiths, a symbol of peace and innocence.

Mourning doves, Jewish Hill

BOOK. While most often signifying the Bible, it may also denote the Book of Life. An open book signifies someone with an open heart or open feelings. A closed book represents a life completed.

Open book, Original Six Acres

BUTTERFLY. A butterfly or chrysalis signifies death and rebirth.

CHAIN OR CHAIN LINKS. Signifies life or a family circle. A broken chain symbolizes the breaking of the chain by death.

CIRCLE. Signifies eternity.

COLUMN. Symbolizes commemoration. A broken column denotes a life cut short.

CROSS. The most universally identified symbol of Christian faith and belief in salvation. There are several styles of crosses. Among those found at Oakland are the following:

Cross of Calvary. A Latin Cross with three equal sections signifying faith, hope, and love.

Celtic cross. Often ornately carved; the circle around the center symbolizes eternity. This cross predates the Christian cross.

Saint Andrew's cross. Often carved on the headstones of Confederate soldiers, this is an emblem of the Stars and Bars battle flag of the Confederacy.

Celtic cross on the Stubbs family lot, Rogers Hill

CROWN. Symbolizes glory after death. Most often found with a Latin cross, their union representing the sovereignty of God.

Cross and crown with knight's head, Bell Tower Ridge

DRAPERY OR SHROUD. Represents sorrow and grief for the lost loved one. On Jewish graves, it often represents a *tallith*, or prayer shawl.

Shroud and urn, Greenhouse Valley

FLAME OR FLAMING TORCH. Represents spiritual immortality. An upright torch symbolizes life, while an inverted torch represents life extinguished.

Inverted torch on Burke vault, Original Six Acres

FLOWERS AND PLANTS. Represent both the beauty and frailty of life. A broken flower indicates a life terminated. Particular flowers may have distinct meanings. Examples include:

Calla Lily. Marriage and fidelity.

Daisy. Innocence.

Easter Lily. Innocence and purity (virginity). It was often used to represent death at an early age.

Fern. Humility, sincerity, and solitude.

Fleur-de-Lis. Purity and eternity.

Lily of the Valley. Innocence and purity. As one of the first flowers of spring, it also signifies renewal.

Lotus. An Egyptian symbol of creation and a Christian symbol of perfection and purity.

Morning Glory. Christ's Resurrection, because the flower opens in the morning and closes in the afternoon.

Pansy. Humility and remembrance.

Passion Flower. The Passion of Christ, because of the flower's structure and life cycle.

Poppy. Sleep and death.

Rose. Love and life. A rosebud signifies an infant or child death; a broken stem, a life cut short; a rose in full bloom, a long life.

Tulip. Charity and love.

Roses carved in monument, Greenhouse Valley

GARLAND OR WREATH OF FLOWERS.
An ancient symbol of victory. In Christian imagery, it represents victory over death.

HAND. A hand may have multiple interpretations.

Pointing down. Symbolizes God reaching down from heaven.

Pointing up. Signifies that the soul has gone up to heaven.

Handshake. If one hand is male and the other female, this denotes matrimony. If the hands are of the same gender, it signifies earthly farewell.

Two hands outstretched. The Jewish "raising the hands" blessing. It may also symbolize the *Kohen,* descendants of Aaron and the high priests of the Temple in Jerusalem.

Heart in the palm of the hand. Symbolizes love and faithfulness.

Clasped hands, Knit Mill

HEART. A symbol of love. A heart encircled with thorns represents the suffering of Christ.

IVY. The leaves and vines symbolize eternal attachment, affection, and friendship.

LAMB. A symbol of innocence. In the Christian tradition, it represents Christ, the Paschal sacrifice. The symbol is most often seen on the graves of children.

Bryant lambs, Original Six Acres

LION. Signifies power, strength, courage, and fidelity.

LOGS. A grave monument in the shape of logs often signified that the deceased was associated with the Woodmen of the World (note that the organization's symbol will be part of the monument). Small logs indicate the grave of a child.

Woodmen of the World symbols, Original Six Acres

MENORAH. This seven-branched candlestick symbolizes the seven days of creation and God's divine presence.

MOURNING FIGURE. Symbolizes sorrow and grief. These figures gained popularity in the early twentieth century.

OBELISK. Its use was popularized by Victorians, who were influenced by archaeological discoveries in Egypt. The shaft denoted power.

RINGS. Represents the circle of family. A broken ring symbolizes the breaking of the circle through death.

ROCK. A symbol of strength and stability. A pile of rocks indicates "a life begun on a firm Christian foundation."

SAINTS. Statues or carvings of saints often signify the deceased's plea for the saint's care and benevolence (most notable are St. Joseph, St. John, St. Anthony, and St. Cecilia).

Effigy of St. Anthony and child, Bell Tower Ridge

SHELL. A pre-Christian symbol representing fertility and the womb. Most often associated with children's graves.

Nedom Angier obelisk, Bell Tower Ridge

Seashell and reclining child figure, Bell Tower Ridge

SKULL. Represents death. A winged skull signifies the soul's flight to heaven (more popular in pre-Victorian graves).

STAR. Signifies heaven. Star types may have other meanings:

Four-pointed star. A representation of the cross.

Five-pointed star. Epiphany or heavenly wisdom.

Six-pointed star. Star of David, formed by super-imposing two triangles. In Judaism, it represents the Magen David, or Shield of David.

Seven-pointed star. Seven gifts of the Holy Spirit.

Nine-pointed star. Nine fruits of the Holy Spirit.

Star of David, Jewish Flat

TREE. A tree symbolizes life; a stump signifies a life cut short. Particular trees may have distinct meanings. Examples include:

Acanthus. Peace in the Garden of Eden.

Dogwood. The crucifixion of Christ (according to legend, dogwood timber was used for the cross), the Resurrection, and eternal life. Because of its shape and markings, a dogwood blossom symbolizes the Crucifixion, too.

Laurel. Worldly accomplishment, heroism, or victory; usually found formed into a wreath.

Oak. Strength, power, endurance, virtue, honor, and faith.

Palm. Christ's triumphal entry into Jerusalem, death on the cross, and the promise of Resurrection.

Willow. Sorrow and mourning, in both the Christian and Jewish traditions.

Broken willow symbol, Old Jewish Burial Ground in Original Six Acres

URN. A pre-Christian symbol of immortality (in ancient Egypt, vital organs of the deceased were stored in urn-like jars). An urn with a flame represents undying remembrance.

VESSEL OR LAMP WITH FLAME. Represents eternity and the eternal spirit.

Lamp and flame in stained glass, Elsas mausoleum, Jewish Hill

WHEAT. Usually shown as a sheaf, it signifies the bread of the Last Supper, as well as a long and fruitful life.

Appendix B

Numerical Sections Map of Oakland Cemetery for Burial Records Research

THE USE OF descriptive titles for the different sections of Oakland Cemetery is a relatively new feature. In the historical burial records used by the sexton's office and the Historic Oakland Foundation as well as families, genealogists, and researchers, burial site locations are identified by a numerical system that maps areas of the cemetery. The block and lot numbers found throughout this guide are the same in both the descriptive and numerical systems. For readers interested in researching burial records at Oakland, the numerical sections map is below. (Note: The numbers 13 and 19 were not used in identifying cemetery sections in the historical burial records, so they have been omitted from this map.)

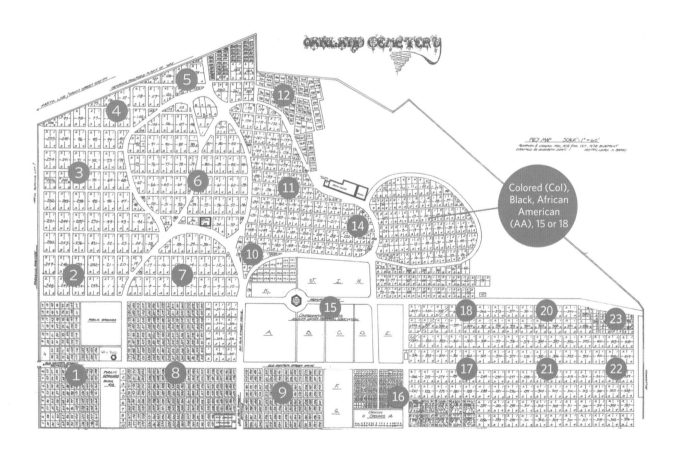

Appendix C

State and City Leaders Buried at Oakland

Members of the United States Congress

NAME	TERM	BURIAL LOCATION
John B. Gordon (d. 1904) (see also Georgia Governors)	1873–80 (Senate); 1891–97 (Senate)	Confederate Memorial Grounds, Block K-3
Benjamin H. Hill (d. 1882)	1875–77 (House); 1877–82 (Senate)	Rogers Hill, Block 315
Joseph E. Brown (d. 1894) (see also Georgia Governors)	1880–91 (Senate)	Knit Mill, Block 99
M. Hoke Smith (d. 1931) (see also Georgia Governors)	1911–21 (Senate)	Rogers Hill, Block 303
Lucius J. Gartrell (d. 1891)	1857–61 (House)	Knit Mill, Block 47

Georgia Governors

NAME	TERM	BURIAL LOCATION
Joseph E. Brown (d. 1894)	1857–65	Knit Mill, Block 99
Alexander H. Stephens (d. 1883)	1882–83	Body relocated to Liberty Hall in 1884
John B. Gordon (d. 1904)	1886–90	Confederate Memorial Grounds, Block K-3
William J. Northen (d. 1913)	1890–94	Confederate Memorial Grounds, Block LM-18
M. Hoke Smith (d. 1931)	1907–9	Rogers Hill, Block 303
Joseph M. Brown (d. 1932)	1909–11; 1912–13	Knit Mill, Block 99
John M. Slaton (d. 1955)	1913–15	Bell Tower Ridge, Block 57

Atlanta Mayors

NAME	TERM	BURIAL LOCATION
Moses Formwalt (d. 1852)	1848–49	Bell Tower Ridge, Block 11
Benjamin F. Bomar (d. 1868)	1849–50	Original Six Acres, Blocks 84–85
Willis Buell (d. 1851)	1850–51	Location unknown
Jonathan Norcross (d. 1898)	1851–52	Greenhouse Valley, Block 140
John F. Mims (d. 1856)	1853	Original Six Acres, Block 217
William Markham (d. 1890)	1853–54	Bell Tower Ridge, Block 8
John Glen (d. 1895)	1855–56	Original Six Acres, Block 337
William Ezzard (d. 1887)	1856–58; 1860–61; 1870–71	Original Six Acres, Block 208
Jared Whitaker (d. 1884)	1861	Bell Tower Ridge, Block 7
Thomas Lowe (d. 1875)	1861–62	Original Six Acres, Block 435
James Calhoun (d. 1875)	1862–66	Original Six Acres, Block 395
James E. Williams (d. 1900)	1866–69	Original Six Acres, Block 415
William H. Hulsey (d. 1909)	1869–70	Knit Mill, Block 98
Samuel B. Spencer (d. 1901)	1874–75	Hogpen Corner, Block 727
Nedom Angier (d. 1882)	1877–79	Bell Tower Ridge, Block 13
William L. Calhoun (d. 1908)	1879–81	Original Six Acres, Block 384
James W. English (d. 1925)	1881–83	Bell Tower Ridge, Block 52
George Hillyer (d. 1931)	1885–87	Knit Mill, Block 254
John Tyler Cooper (d. 1912)	1887–89	Bell Tower Ridge, Block 56
John T. Glenn (d. 1899)	1889–91	Original Six Acres, Block 341
William Hemphill (d. 1902)	1891–93	Knit Mill, Block 73
Porter King (d. 1901)	1895–97	Original Six Acres, Block 393
Charles A. Collier (d. 1900)	1897–99	Bell Tower Ridge, Block 30
James G. Woodward (d. 1923)	1899–1901; 1905–7; 1913–17	Original Six Acres, Block 410
Robert F. Maddox Jr. (d. 1965)	1909–10	Bell Tower Ridge, Block 56
Ivan Allen Jr. (d. 2003)	1962–70	Rogers Hill, Block 296
Maynard H. Jackson (d. 2003)	1974–82; 1990–94	North Public Grounds

Appendix D

A Selection of Oakland Cemetery's Tours and Annual Events

ALL YEAR. Volunteer-led weekend walking tours. Private group tours by appointment.

FEBRUARY. Special tours of the African American Grounds during Black History Month.

MARCH. A selection of tours offered as part of the Atlanta Preservation Center's Phoenix Flies Celebration. Full schedule of general and themed walking tours, including weekend twilight tours (mid-March through October).

APRIL. Annual UDC Commemoration of Confederate Memorial Day.

MAY. Tunes from the Tombs: A Weekend of Music and Spirits.

OCTOBER. Sunday in the Park: A Victorian Festival (first Sunday). Run Like Hell (5K) Race and Run Like Heck (1K) Fun Run. Capturing the Spirit of Oakland Halloween Tours.

For details on these events and other scheduled programs and activities, contact the Historic Oakland Foundation: 404–688–2107, www.oaklandcemetery.com

Notes

Introduction

1. Kennedy, *Ironweed*, 3.
2. See Albany Diocesan Cemeteries, accessed August 25, 2011, http://www.rcdacemeteries.org/albany_catholic_cemeteries.html#stagnes.
3. Yalom, *American Resting Place*, 45; French, "The Cemetery as Cultural Institution," 45.
4. Story, *An Address Delivered on the Dedication of the Cemetery at Mount Auburn*, 29.
5. Ibid., 16–17.
6. Ibid., 17.
7. *New York Daily Tribune*, June 5, 1850.
8. Downing, *Rural Essays*, 154.
9. Yalom, *American Resting Place*, 46.
10. Downing, *Rural Essays*, 142.
11. French, "Cemetery as Cultural Institution," 56–59.
12. Downing, *Rural Essays*, 157.
13. Ibid., 158–59.
14. *Atlanta Constitution*, May 31, 1871.
15. Ibid., June 17, 1883.
16. Ibid., October 26, 1869.
17. Ibid., April 26, 1890.
18. Ibid., June 30, 1870.
19. Ibid., April 28, 1896.
20. Blight, *Race and Reunion*, 65–96.
21. *Atlanta Constitution*, April 28, 1896.
22. Ibid., July 29, 1936; April 21, 1938.
23. Ibid., April 21, 1938, 1.
24. Crimmins and Farrisee, *Democracy Restored*, 82–87.
25. *Atlanta Constitution*, April 27, 1938.
26. Ibid., March 9, 1883.
27. Ibid., June 4, 1885.
28. Ibid., December 26, 1889.
29. Ibid., February 5, 1892.
30. Ibid., April 18, 1882.
31. Ibid., April 22, 1883.
32. Ibid., September 26, 1884.
33. Beard, "Hurt's Deserted Village," 200–201; *Atlanta Constitution*, February 19, 1890.
34. Downing, *Rural Essays*, 142.
35. *Atlanta Daily World*, June 25, 1934; August 17, 1934; February 13, 1934; February 26, 1934; January 30, 1938; June 12, 1940.
36. *Atlanta Constitution*, June 27, 2003.

ONE. *From Atlanta Cemetery to Historic Oakland: A Short History*

Epigraph quoted in Robbie Brown, "Atlanta Saves Battered Gem, a Home for the Dead That's Prized by the Living," *New York Times*, October 11, 2008, http://nytimes.com/2008/10/11/us/11cemetery.html.

1. Garrett, *Atlanta and Environs*, 1:315.
2. Ibid.
3. Quoted in Moore, "Atlanta's Pride and Problem," 19.
4. Yalom, *American Resting Place*, 29.
5. Barnwell, *Barnwell's Atlanta City Directory*, 1:25.
6. Faust, *Republic of Suffering*, 81.
7. In Zaworski, *Headstones of Heroes*, 7, quoting Wright's letter as recorded in the National Archives and Records Administration, Record Group 109, chapter 2, volume 186, *Military Departments, Letters Sent, Commander of Troops at Atlanta, July 1863–May 1864*, 59–60.
8. *War of the Rebellion*, 777.
9. Faust, *Republic of Suffering*, xii.

10. Moore, "Atlanta's Pride and Problem," quoting Samuel Pierce Richards (who was quoting Mayor Calhoun), diary entry for September 17, 1865 (Atlanta History Center Collection).

11. Faust, *Republic of Suffering*, 149.

12. Barksdale, "Our Confederate Dead," 98, quoting Alberta Malone, *History of the Atlanta Ladies Memorial Association, 1866–1946: Markers and Monuments* (Atlanta, 1946), 68.

13. Zaworski, *Headstones of Heroes*, 9.

14. Garrett, *Atlanta and Environs*, 1:852.

15. Mrs. George Fry, "A Labor of Love: The History of the Atlanta Memorial Association Told by Mrs. George T. Fry; Heroic Conduct of the Southern Ladies," *Atlanta Constitution*, April 26, 1890.

16. McKinley, *Speeches and Addresses of William McKinley*, 158.

17. Downing, *Rural Essays*, 154.

18. Combs, "All That Live Must Hear," 93.

19. Williams, *Echoes from the Battlefield*, 59.

20. Quoted in Moore, "Atlanta's Pride and Problem," 29.

21. Quoted in ibid.

22. Quoted in ibid., 30.

23. Quoted in ibid., 33.

24. Ibid., 35.

25. Quoted in ibid., 35.

26. Quoted in Garrett, *Atlanta and Environs*, 1:739.

27. William Neal, "Census of the Dead," *Atlanta Journal*, July 11, 1937.

28. Chuck Bell, "Oakland Links Atlanta to Past," *Atlanta Constitution*, September 24, 1975.

29. Brown, "Atlanta Saves a Battered Gem."

30. Karl W. Ritzler, "Why I Love My Job: Kevin Kuharic, Director of Restoration, Oakland Cemetery," *Atlanta Journal-Constitution*, October 26, 2008, http://ajc.com/ajccars/content/hotjobs/careercenter/articles/2008/10/26/cooljobs_oaklandcem.html.

31. Ibid.

TWO. *Historic Oakland and the Elements of the Rural Garden Cemetery Movement*

Epigraph taken from Combs, "All That Live Must Hear," 61.

1. Rutherford, *Victorian Cemetery*, 29.

2. Downing, *Rural Essays*, 154.

3. Waterhouse, *Sacred Symbols of Oakland*, xx.

4. Quoted in Walker, "Iconography & Epitaphs," Note: This website was disabled while this book was being written; a printout of the information is available in the archives of the Historic Oakland Foundation.

5. J. Joseph Edgette, "The Epitaph and Personality Revelation," in Meyer, *Cemeteries and Grave-markers*, 101.

6. Ariès, *Hour of Our Death*, 78.

7. Edgette, "Epitaph and Personality Revelation," 88–89.

THREE. *Exploring Oakland Cemetery: A Tour by Sections*

Epigraph taken from Keister, *Stories in Stone*, 11.

FOUR. *A Gathering Place: Oakland Cemetery's Vital Role in the Atlanta Community*

Epigraph taken from Downing, *Rural Essays*, 157.

1. Keister, *Forever Dixie*, 10.

2. Ibid.

3. Mueller, "Two Hundred Years of Memorialization," 22.

4. Ibid.

5. Quoted in Garrett, *Atlanta and Environs*, II:16.

Selected Sources

Ariès, Philippe. *The Hour of Our Death: The Classic History of Western Attitudes toward Death over the Last One Thousand Years.* Translated by Helen Weaver. New York: Vintage, 1982.

Barksdale, Richard Harwell. "Our Confederate Dead." *Atlanta Historical Bulletin* 20, no. 2 (Summer 1976): 97–109.

Barnwell, V. T. *Barnwell's Atlanta City Directory and Stranger's Guide.* Volume I. Atlanta: Intelligencer Book and Job Office, 1867.

Beard, Rick. "Hurt's Deserted Village: Atlanta's Inman Park, 1885–1911." In *Olmsted South: Old South Critic, New South Planner,* ed. Dana F. White and Victor Kramer, 195–221. Westport, Conn.: Greenwood, 1979.

Berry, Carrie. Diary. Original in the Atlanta History Center Collection; also available at http://americancivilwar.com/women/carrie_berry.html.

Blight, David W. *Race and Reunion: The Civil War in American Memory.* Cambridge, Mass.: Harvard University Press, 2001.

Bowlby, Elizabeth Catherine. "The Role of Atlanta during the Civil War." MA thesis, Emory University, 1939.

Clayton, Sarah Conley. *Requiem for a Lost City: A Memoir of Civil War Atlanta and the Old South.* Macon, Ga.: Mercer University Press, 1999.

Combs, Diana Williams. "All That Live Must Hear." *Atlanta Historical Bulletin* 20, no. 2 (Summer 1976): 61–95.

Crimmins, Timothy J., and Anne Farrisee. *Democracy Restored: A History of the Georgia Capitol.* Athens: University of Georgia Press, 2007.

Dickens, Roy, and Blakely, Robert. "Preliminary Report on Archeological Investigation in Oakland Cemetery, Atlanta, Georgia." Paper presented at the Conference on Historic Site Archeology, Institute of Archeology and Anthropology, University of South Carolina, 1979.

Downing, Andrew Jackson. *Rural Essays.* New York: Putnam, 1853.

Faust, Drew Gilpin. *This Republic of Suffering: Death and the American Civil War.* New York: Knopf, 2008.

Foster, Margaret. "Atlanta Cemetery Repaired after Tornado." *Preservation,* November 10, 2008. http://www.preservationnation.org/magazine/2008/todays-news/atlanta-cemetery-repaired.html.

French, Stanley. "The Cemetery as Cultural Institution: The Establishment of Mount Auburn and the 'Rural Cemetery' Movement." *American Quarterly* 26 (March 1974): 37–59.

Fryman, Robert J. "Bio-Archeological Investigation of the Unassigned Section (Potters' Field), Oakland Cemetery, Atlanta, Georgia." Report to Mitchell Construction Company by Blue Arrow Research, June 1999.

Galphin, Bruce, and Norman Shavin. *Atlanta: Triumph of a People.* Atlanta: Capricorn, 1982.

Garrett, Franklin M. *Atlanta and Environs: A Chronicle of Its People and Events.* Volumes I and II. New York: Lewis Historical, 1954. Facsimile reprint, Athens: University of Georgia Press, 1969.

———. "Note and Document: Historic Oakland Cemetery A Tangible Link to Atlanta's Past." *Atlanta History: A Journal of Georgia and the South* 32, no. 1 (Spring 1988): 42–61.

———. "Oakland Cemetery: An Irreplaceable Aid to Historical and Genealogical Research." *Atlanta Historical Bulletin* 20, no. 2 (Summer 1976): 7–12.

Georgia Department of Natural Resources, Historic Preservation Division. *Preserving Georgia's Historic Cemeteries.* 2007.

Griffith, Joe. "Joe Brown's Pikes: Southern Cold Steel in Close Quarters." *Journal of the Historical Society of the Georgia National Guard* 8, no. 2 (2000): 6–12. http://www.hsgng.org/pages/joebrownpike.htm.

Henderson, Alexa Benson. "Paupers, Pastors and Politicians: Reflections Upon Afro-Americans Buried at Oakland Cemetery." *Atlanta Historical Bulletin* 20, no. 2 (Summer 1976): 43–60.

Hertzberg, Steven. *Strangers within the Gate City: The Jews of Atlanta, 1845–1915*. Philadelphia: Jewish Publication Society of America, 1978.

Historic Oakland Cemetery Foundation. *City of Stone: A Guide to the Mausolea at Atlanta's Oldest Cemetery*. (Internal document, ca. 1992; not published for public use.)

———. *A Guide to the Black Section*. (Internal document, 1990s; not published for public use.)

———. *A Guide to the Confederate Section*. (Internal document, 1990s; not published for public use.)

———. *A Guide to the Jewish Sections*. (Internal document, ca. 1992; not published for public use.)

Historic Oakland Cemetery, Inc. "Report of First Annual Meeting." April 24, 1977.

Historic Oakland News. Various issues, 1989–93.

Jewish Federation of Greater Atlanta. *L'Chaim: The History of Jews in Atlanta*. Atlanta: Bookhouse, 2006.

Kaemmerlen, Cathy J. *The Historic Oakland Cemetery of Atlanta: Speaking Stones*. Charleston: History Press, 2007.

Keister, Douglas. *Forever Dixie: A Field Guide to Southern Cemeteries and Their Residents*. Salt Lake City: Gibbs Smith, 2008.

———. *Stories in Stone: A Field Guide to Cemetery Symbolism and Iconography*. Salt Lake City: Gibbs Smith, 2004.

Kennedy, William. *Ironweed: A Novel*. New York: Penguin, 1983.

Making of America: Georgia Edition. Volumes I and IV. Atlanta: Caldwell, 1912.

McKinley, William. *Speeches and Addresses of William McKinley: From March 1, 1897, to May 30, 1900*. New York: Doubleday and McClure, 1900.

Meyer, Richard E., ed. *Cemeteries and Gravemarkers: Voices of American Culture*. Logan: Utah State University Press, 1989.

Moore, Kent. "Atlanta's Pride and Problem." *Atlanta Historical Bulletin* 20, no.2 (Summer 1976): 19–41.

Morley, John. *Death, Heaven, and the Victorians*. Pittsburgh: University of Pittsburgh Press, 1971.

Mueller, Eileen. "Two Hundred Years of Memorialization." *Monument Builder News*, July 1976, 6–50.

New Georgia Encyclopedia. http://www.georgiaencyclopedia.org/nge/Home.jsp.

Reid, Pam. "Cemetery Art and Symbolism." *Ancestry*, September 1, 2000. http://learn.ancestry.com/LearnMore/Article.aspx?id=2977.

Reynolds, William J. "B. F. White: The Sacred Harp Man." *Sacred Harp Singing in Texas*. http://biographies.texasfasola.org/bfwhite.html.

Rutherford, Sarah. *The Victorian Cemetery*. Oxford: Shire, 2009.

Story, Joseph. *An Address Delivered on the Dedication of the Cemetery at Mount Auburn*. Boston: Buckingham, 1831.

Taliaferro, Tevi. *Historic Oakland Cemetery*. Mount Pleasant, S.C.: Arcadia, 2001.

Walker, Marlene Koon. "Iconography and Epitaphs" www.palmettoroots.org/tombstones.html. Note: The website was disabled while this book was being written; a printout of the information is available in the archives of the Historic Oakland Foundation.

The War of the Rebellion: A Compilation of the Official Records of the Union and Confederate Armies; Series I, Volume 38 (Part V). Washington, D.C.: United States War Department, 1891.

Waterhouse, Richard. *Sacred Symbols of Oakland: A Guide to the Many Sacred Symbols of Atlanta's Oldest Public Cemetery*. Conover, N.C.: Goosepen Studio & Press, 2010.

Williams, Noble Calhoun. *Echoes From the Battlefield; or, Southern Life during the War*. Atlanta: Franklin Printing, 1902.

Yalom, Marilyn. *The American Resting Place: Four Hundred Years of History through Our Cemeteries and Burial Grounds*. New York: Houghton Mifflin Harcourt, 2008.

Zaworski, Robert E. *Headstones of Heroes: The Restoration and History of Confederate Graves in Atlanta's Oakland Cemetery*. Paducah, Ky.: Turner, 1998.

Illustration Credits

All photographs are by Ren Davis except as noted below.

Ivan Allen Jr. family
>Page 135 (Allen portrait)

Atlanta History Center, Kenan Research Center
>Pages xxii, xxviii, xxix, 22, 23, 26, 27 (letter), 78 (Mitchell portrait), 109, 124,
>176 (Confederate Memorial Day, ca. 1901), and 177 (birthday announcement)

City of Atlanta (Oakland Sexton's Office)
>Pages 66 (Calhoun portrait), 68 (Austell portrait), 80 (Brown portrait), 108 (Gordon portrait),
>110 (Northen portrait), 113 (Milledge and Evans portraits), 136 (Hill portrait), 152 (Butler portrait),
>153, 155 (Graves portrait), 156 (Gaines portrait), 156 (Rucker portrait), and 157 (Quarles portrait)

Timothy J. Crimmins
>Pages xix, xxxi, and xxxii

Georgia Archives
>Pages 25, 28, 82, 96 (Slaton portrait), and 110 (Northen in Fitzgerald)

Historic Oakland Foundation
>Pages 5, 14, 17, 20, 21, 29 (both), 33, 56, 79 (Hurt portrait), 96 (Maddox portrait), 122 (Jones portrait),
>125 (Rich portrait), 126 (Elsas portrait), 139 (Westmoreland portrait), 178, and 192

Valerie Jackson
>Page 70 (Jackson portrait)

Library of Congress
>Pages 13 and 177 (bird's-eye-view map)

Mount Auburn Illustrated
>Pages xv, xvi, xvii, and xxi

National Archives and Records Administration
>Page 12

State Bar of Georgia
>Page 95 (Bleckley portrait)

United Daughters of the Confederacy, Alfred H. Colquitt Chapter
>Page 176 (Confederate Memorial Day, ca. 1870s)

Mary Woodlan
>Pages 36 and 37

Index

Historic Oakland Foundation

THE MISSION of the Historic Oakland Foundation is to partner with the City of Atlanta to preserve, restore, enhance, and share Oakland Cemetery with the public as an important cultural resource and an island of tranquility in the heart of the city. The foundation was founded in 1976, the same year that Oakland Cemetery was placed on the National Register of Historic Places.

The foundation plans and oversees restoration, raises funds, provides educational programs and activities, manages marketing and publicity, promotes membership, recruits and manages volunteers, plans and executes special events, and operates a visitors center. Specific educational programs and activities include guided tours organized around various themes, including the Civil War, pioneers of Atlanta, and Victorian symbolism at Oakland Cemetery. These tours serve as an important educational resource for public and private school systems throughout the South. Family events such as Tunes from the Tombs, the Sunday in the Park Victorian festival, Capturing the Spirit of Oakland Halloween tours, and the Run Like Hell 5K Road Race draw thousands of participants every year.

To attract visitors and remain a valuable community resource, the foundation works diligently to maintain Oakland Cemetery's natural beauty, artistic splendor, and historical integrity. This requires year-round restoration and preservation efforts. Working from a master plan, including a ten-phase plan for restoration and preservation, the foundation is steadily and systematically restoring the mausoleums, monuments, grave markers, sculptures, walls, and walkways contained in this forty-eight-acre cultural and historic landmark. Landscaping activities are aligned with strategies and guidelines in our Historic Landscape Restoration Plan for Oakland Cemetery.

The Historic Oakland Foundation is a not-for-profit, 501(c)(3) charitable organization. Donations to the foundation are critical to the continued preservation of historic Oakland Cemetery. To learn more or to join us in our continuing work to restore and preserve Historic Oakland, please contact us.

The Historic Oakland Foundation
www.oaklandcemetery.com
248 Oakland Avenue
Atlanta, GA 30312
(404) 688–2107